THE SPLENDOUR OF
THE PREACHERS

Duncan Macpherson

The Splendour of the Preachers

New approaches to Liturgical Preaching

ST PAULS

ST PAULS Publishing
187 Battersea Bridge Road, London SW11 3AS, UK
www.stpaulspublishing.com

ISBN 978-0-85439-781-5

A catalogue record is available for this book from the
British Library.

Set by Tukan DTP, Stubbington, Fareham, UK
Printed by Melita Press, Paola, Malta.

ST PAULS is an activity of the priests and brothers
of the Society of St Paul who proclaim the Gospel
through the media of social communication.

Contents

Acknowledgements

Much of the material in this book has been published before in article form and acknowledgements are due to the Tablet Publishing Company for their kind permission to reprint articles which appeared in *The Pastoral Review* and which are reprinted here with minor alterations. The first sections of the first four chapters of this book substantially reproduce a series of four articles entitled *Proclaiming the Word at Mass*: 1. Heralds of the Word, *The Pastoral Review,* November/December, 2008; 2. Hearers of the Word, *The Pastoral Review* September/October, 2009; 3. Interpreting the Text, *The Pastoral Review*, March/April, 2009 and 4. Breaking the Word, *The Pastoral Review*, May/June, 2009. Versions of chapters 5-7 were published in *The Pastoral Review* as a series of three articles entitled *Preaching at the Margins, Preaching at Cana* (Preaching at Weddings), *The Pastoral Review*, January/February 2007; *Baptism, The Pastoral Review*, July/August 2007 and *Lazarus is Dead* (Preaching at Funerals), *The Pastoral Review*, March and April 2008. Chapter 8, *Preaching across the ecumenical divide: 'the strange exorcist'* was originally given as a paper for the Annual Meeting of the Academy of Homiletics at Minneapolis in November 2007 and subsequently published in the proceedings of the Academy and a shorter version later in *The Pastoral Review*, January/February 2008.

Acknowledgements are due also to the College of Preachers who published the homily 'Inequitable lives' in *The College of Preachers: the Journal*, July, 2004 and the two homilies illustrating chapter 4 under the heading '*What would Jesus do?*' which were published as sermons for All Saints' Day, in *The College of Preachers' Journal*, July, 2005 and October, 2006. Chapter 9, '*Preaching and the Israeli-Palestinian Conflict: take away the stone*' conflates papers given at the annual Meetings of the Academy of Homiletics, at Boston in 2002 and at West Palm Beach, Florida in 2006 and was previously published in a shorter form in *The Preacher* (formerly the *College of Preachers' Journal*) under the title, 'This Year in Jerusalem', *The Preacher*, April, 2010. A summary of strategies used in the preaching illustrations which follow was published as an appendix to my *Pilgrim Preacher* in the 2004 reprint.

I would also like to thank my friend and former teacher Professor Gregory Heille OP for the foreword to this book and for his advice and encouragement over the years.

Foreword

'Preaching as speaking the Gospel in context'

In *The Splendour of the Preachers*, Deacon Duncan Macpherson has written succinctly and intelligently on the matter of preaching the Christian Gospel particularly in the British context.

For some years now, Doctor Macpherson has brought welcome insight from the British Isles to a most vibrant North American conversation about preaching. Known as the 'New Homiletic', this scholarly body of work, going back some thirty years, has sparked insights about preaching's rhetorical construction *vis-à-vis* the ear of the listener, new approaches to biblical interpretation, the social and liturgical contexts of preaching, and the spirituality and vocation of the preacher.

While on sabbatical at Blackfriars in Oxford, I visited Duncan and his wife Ann and, while being invited into the ecumenical work of the UK College of Preachers, I was able to contribute a lecture at its biennial conference at Swanwick, to give a visiting lecture at Spurgeon's College in London and to join with Duncan in giving a residential course on preaching at All Hallow's College, Dublin. These encounters and conversations have introduced me to the diverse and increasingly lively preaching scene in the United Kingdom and in Ireland. Macpherson's passionate concern for preaching gives Catholic voice to the wonderfully ecumenical arena of British preaching – as evident by his steadfast commitment to the excellent conferences and programmes of the College of Preachers and by his frequent contributions to *The Pastoral Review* and *The Preacher*.

This slim volume provides an excellent primer to both new and seasoned preachers both ordained and lay. Written from both a Roman Catholic and a British context, Macpherson's ecumenical appreciation is evident: I certainly hope this work receives a deserved ecumenical readership. Readers will receive a straightforward presentation of key insights in North American homiletic scholarship, supported by intimate knowledge of British ecclesiastical and social context and made plain in actual homilies given in numerous real contexts. The secular, ecumenical and intercultural contexts of British life are taken seriously and engaged with pastoral intelligence. Macpherson gives simple explanations with examples of current approaches to biblical interpretation. He also explores a variety of current rhetorical approaches to structuring a homily so that its message will be heard and relevant.

Macpherson's longstanding commitment to the plight of Palestinian Christians – both as pilgrimage guide in the Holy Land and as writer of books and articles – makes an appropriate mark in this book as well. Preaching is a political act: always governed by the Gospel message of the Dominion of God, it must steadfastly reflect and address the listeners' social context. Macpherson does this well.

Fr Gregory Heille, OP
Professor of Homiletics and Academic Dean
Aquinas Institute of Theology
Saint Louis, Missouri, U.S.A.

Preface

The name of Jesus is the splendour of preachers because his word is to be proclaimed and heard with glowing splendour...

(St Bernadine of Siena[1])

The homily is 'part of the liturgical action' (139), and is meant to foster a deeper understanding of the word of God, so that it can bear fruit in the lives of the faithful. Hence ordained ministers must 'prepare the homily carefully, based on an adequate knowledge of Sacred Scripture' (140). Generic and abstract homilies should be avoided. In particular, I ask these ministers to preach in such a way that the homily closely relates the proclamation of the word of God to the sacramental celebration.

(Pope Benedict XVI[2])

It is the good news about Jesus which is the splendour of preachers. Their message is the good news that God created us, loves us, and invites us to share his life. By the death and resurrection of Christ the barriers between God and human beings have been broken down and we are freed from sin and death to love God and each other (Eph 1:3-14, 2:13 and 4:32).

The chapters which follow include a number of slightly altered previously published articles all of which were aimed at providing a fresh vision of what preaching involves and what might constitute effective strategies for communicating that vision to the hearers. The first section; 'Proclaiming the Word on Sundays' consists of four chapters concerned with preaching at the Sunday Eucharist. This section is directed at making the homily come alive both in the liturgy and in the life of the people of God. The first chapter is a reflection on the role of the preacher. The remaining chapters focus in turn on the importance of understanding the congregation and its needs, how to interpret the scripture texts in the lectionary and finally on how to communicate the message in the most effective way.

The next section 'Preaching at the margins' consists of chapters which consider approaches to preaching at weddings, infant baptisms and funerals – celebrations at which many in the congregation are on the fringe or completely outside the community of faith. This section also includes the cases of ecumenical preaching and of preaching in the context of pilgrimage.

Many of the chapters conclude with one or more examples of the author's own preaching with homilies selected in order to illustrate the application of some of the issues raised.

SECTION 1
Proclaiming the Word on Sundays

CHAPTER 1

'Frail Earthen Vessels':
Heralds of the Word

But we have this treasure in clay jars, so that it may be made clear that this extraordinary power belongs to God and does not come from us.

(2 Corinthians 4:7)

Believe what you read, teach what you believe and practice what you preach.

(Rite for the Ordination of a Deacon)

The aim of proclamation in the ministry of the Word is to involve the participants in what is heard and to call forth the response of the hearer to the disclosure of God's love. The personality and character of the preacher can have a profound effect upon both the content and the persuasiveness with which this message is preached and the preacher needs to be personally open to the life-transforming power of the good news which he seeks to communicate to others.

Saint Bernadine's emphasis on the name of Jesus as the splendour of preachers is followed by the caution that 'when it is preached it must not be proclaimed by an impure heart or an unclean mouth, but must be kept safe and handed on in a chosen vessel'.[3] There is a wonderful story of how a nineteenth-century Anglican vicar – a man of no great piety – was preaching during a time of evangelical revival. Quite suddenly the words he was uttering overcame him with their power and he broke down in tears. His congregation responded by jumping up and down with glee, shouting, 'The parson's been converted! The parson's been converted!' So preaching is a dangerous business! The preacher not only needs to believe what he reads but to allow it to become his own, through prayer and meditation, identifying a central message of the Gospel for his own life before applying it to his congregation and the people of our times. He must live the message as well as teach it.

Who preaches?

Preaching at mass is only one of the ways in which this good news is proclaimed.[4] Work for peace and social justice, catechesis (whether of adults or children), direct witness to the faith by word or example – all these are examples of ways in which communities and individuals bring God's word to others. However, the proclamation and preaching of the Word in the context of the liturgy is a message primarily orientated towards building up the faith of those who are present in church and who are united by a common faith and baptism.

The ministry of preaching the homily at mass is officially reserved for ordained ministers. Canon Law sees a particular value in the preacher at mass being the chief priest celebrant, but also permits him to entrust the preaching of the homily to a concelebrating priest or, 'according to circumstances, to a deacon' (*Code of Canon Law*, 767).

Suitably qualified laymen and women may be invited to preach at word services, at communion services outside of mass or at funeral services where no ordained minister is available, but these permissions seem grudging and fail to acknowledge the positive value of [5] hearing the Word of God refracted through the prism of lay, and – in particular – female lay experience. Pastors sometimes get around the problem by inviting lay people to offer 'reflections' rather than homilies, often presented after Communion.[6]

Whoever the preachers are, they should be conscious of the influences exercised by their personal background and experience. American homileticist Joseph Webb in his *Preaching and the challenge of pluralism* refers to these influences as our negative and positive 'hub symbols'.[7] These derive from our social, educational and cultural background and personal psychology. Thus any preacher needs to discern how to use personal experience in ways that communicate conviction without distracting the congregation away from a Christ-centred message towards the preacher's own personality, preferences and prejudices.

The preacher as 'mediator of meaning'

In order to get the personal background of the preacher into a proper context, the preacher needs a clear understanding and model of what it means to be a preacher. The preacher can be seen as herald, pastor or storyteller.[8] The post-Vatican II model of preaching marks a transition of emphasis from the preacher as teacher, instructing in the faith, to one of herald, proclaiming a Christ-centred message of God's saving intervention in history.[9] Taken seriously, this should exclude the riding of hobbyhorses and preaching 'off the text'. Nevertheless the preacher's own faith experience does not exclude the relevance or the need for the preacher to be a listener – a listener to the word of God and a listener to the people that he serves. According to the American bishops' conference document on preaching, *Fulfilled in your hearing*, the preacher is 'the mediator of meaning, representing both the community and the Lord'.[10] In order to be such a mediator, the preacher needs 'to be a listener before he is a speaker'.[11]

The role of 'mediator of meaning' does not exclude the role of teacher. The homily needs to be both catechetical *and* kerygmatic since the primary affective aim of a liturgical homily requires the support of secondary cognitive objectives. In other words, proclamation may require the backing of sound teaching. Pope John Paul II stressed the importance of the homily not only as liturgical and biblical and tailored to the needs of the congregation (the description favoured by Pope Paul VI in the encyclical *Evangelii nuntiandi*, 43), but also as bringing 'catechetical fruits'. The Catechism, too, stresses the instructional value of the homily while at the same time defining the homily as an exhortation to accept the Word 'as what it truly is, the Word of God as put into practice'.[12]

Inevitably there can be tensions between the roles of herald and teacher. In some parts of the Catholic world programmes of doctrinal instruction have been suggested structured around the lectionary. However this runs the risk of the scriptural and liturgical character of the homily being obscured and the texts of Scripture being used as a springboard for talking about unrelated matters. Other solutions to the need for systematic religious instruction include provision for a brief religious instruction by any suitably qualified person after the communion. Another suggestion is that the teaching should emerge naturally from the preaching of biblical and liturgical texts.

Whatever the balance between roles, the preacher

needs to realise that he is not proclaiming his own message but Christ. In consequence, he needs competence in biblical scholarship and rootedness in the tradition of the Church, 'nourished by profound meditation upon the inspired Word, the exegesis of the fathers, conciliar documents and the teaching of the Magisterium'.[13] Subject to individual gifts and circumstances, every preacher should endeavour to find his own optimum level as a student of biblical and theological studies.

Fulfilled in your hearing stressed that the preacher should also have a background in the cultural world in which he preaches; both at the level of great literature and art and also at the popular level. He should seek to understand the 'complex social, political and economic forces' that shape events. 'As long as we carry the Word of God with us, a Word that we have allowed to touch on our lives in prayer and reflection, and as long as we speak that word in language and images that are familiar to the dwellers of the particular avenue we are travelling, the Word of God will be preached, and the possibility of faith and conversion will be present.' For those who find the task described daunting, the document adds that preachers do not need to have all the answers and cites a survey in which what the majority of respondents 'wanted was simply to hear a person of faith preaching'.[14] The role of the preacher as witness needs to be added to that of herald, teacher and mediator of meaning.[15]

'A person of faith preaching'

This raises the question of how much 'a person of faith' who is witness to the truth the Word that he preaches should refer to his own faith and life in order to illuminate the message. Some American Protestant homileticists strongly advocate autobiographical preaching.[16] This advocacy has roots in the Evangelical tradition of offering 'personal testimony'. There are occasions when the preacher can and should describe his own experience by way of illustration and the great American pioneer of the new homiletic, David Buttrick, probably goes too far when he rules out such personal preaching entirely.[17] Maybe the occasions when a strongly personal note is appropriate are few and far between, but they do exist.

Paul, Augustine and Newman were all great autobiographical writers who related their faith to written personal story. We possess no examples of Paul preaching at a Eucharist. What we do have is the writing in his epistles and – at least as refracted by Luke – his speeches in Acts. On the other hand we do possess a good number of sermons by Augustine and Newman and they offer no examples of autobiographical preaching. Indeed, for either of these two giants of preaching *and* of autobiography, to tell their own story when preaching liturgically would have been completely out of character. This does not to mean that their personal ethos did not permeate every word that either of them preached. The personally authentic does not need to be strictly autobiographical. Not everything in the story of a preacher's life is either edifying or interesting. On the other hand, the fact that the Gospel message finds a correspondence in the personality and conviction of the preacher *is* edifying and, indeed, crucial. Occasionally this will legitimise personal anecdote but not often. Buttrick remains nearer the mark. The people of God know when the preacher really believes the message without too much self-referencing.

Pope Saint Gregory the Great (c.540-604) offers a good illustration of how the personality and character of the preacher can have a profound effect upon the both the content and the persuasiveness of preaching. Gregory was forced to leave his monastic life to become a deacon, administering the affairs of the Roman Church. He became papal legate to Constantinople before becoming pope in 590. As pope he became increasingly involved in confronting the severe problems facing both the church and society at the time. In one homily Gregory spells out publicly his personal history, examining his conscience on the humbling relationship between the words he preaches and his own life: 'when I speak, it is myself I am reproaching. I do not preach as I should nor does my life follow the principles I preach so inadequately.'[18]

First steps

The preacher who seeks both to preach as he should and to follow the principles he preaches should be able to discern his own 'hub symbols'. His first step in preaching preparation should then consist in identifying the message he has already made his own through prayer and meditation. This should precede any reading of commentaries or sermon outlines or discussion of the passage with others. A central message that can be expressed in one clear sentence should emerge. This message can then provide the basis for the structure of the rest of the homily, developing in the light of further study – of the congregation, the text and the appropriate preaching strategies to mediate the good news of Jesus Christ, the 'splendour of preachers'.

First Preaching Application:
'Woe betide me if I do not proclaim the Gospel.'

The homily which follows was preached on the Fifth Sunday in Ordinary Time in Year B. The readings used and referred to in the homily were Job 7:1-4,6-7, 1 Corinthians 9:16-19, 22-23 and Mark 1:29-39. The congregation age, social and education background was very mixed but some of those of first or second generation Irish background would generally have the attitude to preaching that a good homily was a very short one.

The central message that emerged could be expressed in the sentence: 'We are all called to be preachers but we cannot do it in our own power.'

Quite coincidentally, some of the key insights of this chapter emerge in the text of this homily. The homily also illustrates the extent and the limits to which the preacher can usefully bring himself to use autobiography in his preaching. The structure of the homily follows a pattern of problematic, good news and application. The problematic section begins with a 'hook' based on the title line of a dance-pop song written by Brian Elliot, and produced by Stephen Bray and Madonna for her studio album *True Blue* in 1986.[19] This is followed by an autobiographical anecdote to illustrate the problem of negative attitudes to preaching. Such attitudes are then contrasted with those of St Paul in 1 Corinthians and of Jesus in the Gospel. The application stresses the universal call to evangelisation founded on an appeal based both upon the generosity of God and the hunger of our sisters and brothers.

Text of the Homily: 'Papa, don't preach me!'

Problematic

'Papa, don't preach me!' In the Catholic Church in this country, preaching is, to say the least, not treated as very important. One day at the church door – not in this church, I am happy to tell you – a man came up to me and said, 'Duncan, I really liked your sermon.' When I asked what it was that he particularly liked I got the answer: 'It was only five minutes long!' What is evident in the Gospel reading you have just heard is that Jesus gives a high priority to preaching. Simon and his companions set out in search of Jesus and when they found him they said, 'Everybody is looking for you.' He answered, 'Let us go elsewhere, to the neighbouring country towns, so that I can preach there too, because that is why I came.'

Like Jesus, Paul in 1 Corinthians, emphasises the importance of preaching, 'If I proclaim the gospel, this gives me no ground for boasting, for an obligation is laid on me, and woe betide me if I do not proclaim the gospel.' Paul is a driven man where preaching is concerned. He doesn't do it for praise. He doesn't do it for money. He does it because he can't help himself. 'Woe to me if I do not preach the Gospel!'

Good News

The reason Paul preaches the good news is to save, to set people free: 'To the weak I became weak, so that I might win the weak. I have become all things to all people, so that I might by any means save some. I do it all for the sake of the gospel, so that I may share in its blessings.' And when Jesus preaches, he heals and he sets people free from possession by devils: 'And the whole city was gathered around the door.[34] And he cured many who were sick with various diseases, and cast out many demons; and he would not permit the demons to speak, because they knew him.'

Application to Liturgy and Life

When we try to apply this to ourselves we need to ask what preaching is, who is called to preach. 'Woe betide me if I do not proclaim the gospel.' First: what is preaching? It is spreading news, spreading good news – news that can save and set free. The point where preaching comes in the Liturgy is the climax of the Liturgy of the Word. Before we go on to the Eucharistic Liturgy to feed on Christ the Word of God under the outward forms of bread and wine, we prepare by feeding on the word of God in Scripture. The homily should help us to digest the word by making the message – or at least part of the message – connect in a realistic way with our lives. A preacher may preach a brilliant rhetorical homily but if it doesn't connect with our lives and the world we live in today then it is a failure. So who is called to preach? The answer is – every baptised Christian. 'An obligation is laid on me, and woe betide me if I do not proclaim the gospel!' Under the present discipline of the Church lay people are not normally permitted to preach at Mass. This is restricted to bishops, priests and deacons. This may change. Some of us think that it should change because otherwise we never get to hear the insights of women Christians at first hand during the Mass. Of course, lay people can be asked to preach at Word Services or at services of Holy Communion outside of Mass. But the word 'preach' has the sense of proclamation and the Word of God that sets people free is not proclaimed only in Church or at services. 'Everyone is searching for you,' the disciples told Jesus. Everybody is still looking for him and it is the responsibility of every disciple of Jesus to help them find him. 'An obligation is laid on me, and woe betide me if I do not proclaim the gospel!'

Whenever we admit to our faith in Christ and try to help someone else to see the connection between that faith and what is going on in their life then we are proclaiming the Word – preaching the Gospel. We are doing it also to by action and example when we act in a caring way, showing to everybody how much difference Christ can make to our lives. 'Woe betide me if I do not proclaim the gospel!'

When we work for social justice or try to bring about peace and to prevent war. 'An obligation is laid on me.' When we follow their example we too are being preachers of the Word. And we can never do this in our own strength or for our own ends. We can do it only by placing ourselves alongside others. Paul says, 'To the weak I became weak, so that I might win the weak. I have become all things to all people, so that I might by any means save some. I do it all for the sake of the gospel, so that I may share in its blessings.' We need to be with other people. We need to be where they are – because that is what God did for us when he became one of us, urgently proclaiming the good news and healing our sickness and driving out evil: 'Let us go on to the neighbouring towns, so that I may proclaim the message there also; for that is what I came out to do. And he went throughout Galilee, proclaiming the message in their synagogues and casting out demons.'

***

Second Preaching Application:
Whom shall I send?

This is an example of narrative preaching based on the Fifth Sunday of the Year with Isaiah 6:1-8; 1 Corinthians 15:1-11; Luke 5:1-11 as the lectionary readings. It was devised for a morning service at a United Reformed church where I, as a Roman Catholic minister, am an ecumenical visiting preacher. Such visits take place two or three times a year, so the preacher and the congregation are well known to each other. The URC congregation of about thirty to forty people is predominantly middle class and middle aged or elderly, plus a few young families. Members of the congregation know the Bible well and are committed and outgoing in their faith. Most have a clearly defined ministry in their church and have a developed consciousness of political and social issues. The challenges facing this community are sometimes dispiriting. I refer to this preaching text as sermon rather than as a homily because it does not take place during a Eucharist or other sacramental rite but serves as the major feature in a service of the Word. The sermon aims to emphasise that all the baptised have been chosen to be apostles without any deserving on their part, because there is work to be done.

Text of the Sermon: 'Head hunted!'

The term 'head-hunter' usually refers to someone who looks for professionals and executives and invites them to apply for jobs they had never thought of applying for. Believe it or not this happened to Fred. He didn't consider himself particularly good at his job – because he wasn't. He tended to daydream in the office, surfing the net, looking at websites that had nothing to do with his work. He could have gone off on courses to improve his work skills, but he was more interested in going to the pub with his mates. So when a head-hunting agency put him in touch with a really plum, interesting and overpaid job, he didn't expect to get it. But he did! Maybe it was the fact that his girlfriend was his previous line manager and it was she who wrote the reference – but he got the job: a six figure salary; a car; foreign travel and the promise of a lot of job satisfaction. But when Fred got the letter of appointment he hesitated. He knew lots of people more suited for the job than he was, but somehow or other he got over his scruples and he took the job.

This emotion of not being the right person to have been chosen was the experience of a personality in all three of the scripture readings we have just heard.

Send me

Isaiah experienced a vision of the awful holiness of God. He could not describe this experience so he used the language of symbol and mystery: 'I saw the Lord sitting on a throne, high and lofty; and the hem of his robe filled the temple...and the house filled with smoke.' And what Isaiah saw made him aware of his own sinfulness: 'Woe is me! I am lost, for I am a man of unclean lips, and I live among a people of unclean lips; yet my eyes have seen the King, the Lord of hosts!' But after the burning coal had touched his lips his sin was taken away and he was able to respond to the call to be God's messenger: 'Whom shall I send, and who will go for us?' He answered, 'Here I am, send me.'

They left everything

In the Gospel, unaided human effort is seen as incapable of bringing in the harvest of fish for which the fishermen are working so laboriously. When the fishermen follow the teaching of Jesus, they pay out their nets and make a fine catch. Like Isaiah, Peter recognises his inadequacy in the presence of divine power and tells Jesus 'Go away from me, Lord, for I am a sinful man!' Like Isaiah he hears the call to be a messenger but Jesus said to Simon Peter, 'Do not be afraid; from now on you will be catching people.' And, like Isaiah he and the other fishermen respond to the call, 'When they had brought their boats to shore, they left everything and followed him.'

Least of the apostles

Everyone who genuinely hears the call to deliver God's message begins and ends with a sense that they are unworthy of the task. Paul, in Corinthians, lists the people who had the awesome experience of encountering the risen Christ and then adds, 'last of all, as to someone untimely born, he appeared also to me. For I am the least of the apostles, unfit to be called an apostle, because I persecuted the church of God…'

Application

Like Fred, like Isaiah, like Peter and the other apostles, including Paul – the one who came last of all, like an unexpected baby to a woman who thought she was past the menopause – each one of us is head-hunted for a job by God.

Some of us may be called to be lay or ordained ministers in our respective churches but we are – all of us – by our common baptism, called to be apostles; to announce the message that every heart is longing to hear. Recognising our own inadequacy, we are able to begin to absorb the wisdom of the teaching that comes from the Christ who comes to meet us as we hear his word this morning. 'I am the least of the apostles, unfit to be called an apostle, because I persecuted the church of God. But by the grace of God I am what I am.'

CHAPTER 2

'The World in Front of the Text: The Hearers of the Word'

'One and the same exhortation does not suit all, inasmuch as neither are all bound together by similarity of character... Therefore according to the quality of the hearers ought the discourses of the teachers to be fashioned, so as to suit all for their several needs and yet never deviate from the art of common edification.'

(St Gregory the Great,
Introduction to Book of Pastoral Rule, III, 1-3)

The first chapter emphasised that the act of preaching and reading is personal, dependent on the gifts and limitations of the preacher. Preaching is also concrete, dependent on the particular situation of those addressed. Exegesis of the congregation is just as important as the exegesis of the Scripture readings and effective preaching requires sensitivity to circumstance, time and community. The question on the mind of the preacher ought to be not just *'what* am I attempting to communicate?' but also, 'who am I preaching for?' Whilst recognising that there are fundamentals common to human beings in every culture, it is essential to identify the variables also. How does the preacher move from the world of the Bible (in history) to a congregation present now? How do we find meaning in biblical texts and relate them to the struggles and concerns, not only of the global community, but also to the life of a congregation in a particular place? It is useful to remember that the ancient 'tradition' of the Church, seen in the Fathers, placed a heavy emphasis on 'allegory' and 'metaphor'. This is the power of symbol working within the pattern of human life, providing numerous parallels between the characters in the Gospel story and experiences of people living today.

In their 1982 document on preaching the American bishops identified three essential elements: the assembly, the preacher and the message itself. They then decided to treat the assembly first, because 'only when preachers know what a congregation needs to hear will they be able to communicate what a congregation needs to hear.'[20] Twenty-six years, later at the 2008 synod of bishops, Bishop Gerald Kicanas of Tucson, vice president of the U.S. episcopal conference, reiterated the same message and urged that after the Church concluded the Jubilee Year of St Paul it should initiate a year dedicated to preaching, providing opportunity for 'priests and deacons with their bishop to meet with the laity to listen to their struggles and to understand better how they might preach the Word in ways that relate to those struggles.'[21]

To relate to such struggles, preachers need to adapt the contents and delivery of the homily both to the congregation and to the wider society in which they live. The interpretation of the biblical message involves making sense of it to cultures very different from that of New Testament times, as well as that of other times and places in the history of the Church. This process, known as 'inculturation', requires sensitivity to the 'world in front of the text' as much as it does to the 'world behind the text.'

This involves translating the message to the changing world and cultures of today as advocated by the Second Vatican Council which urged that methods of teaching should be 'adapted to the needs of the times – to answer, that is, the difficulties and questions that man finds most burdensome and distressing'.[22] This requires that the preacher should understand the culture and the subcultures of the time and place in which he is called to preach. Moreover since human culture and understanding are constantly changing, this requires a constant effort to keep abreast of current events and intellectual movements as well as trends in popular thought and attitudes.

However, the challenge of inculturating the Gospel message through a general understanding of 'the world in front of the text' is not the same as establishing some insight into a specific congregation. Every assembly at every liturgical celebration has a specific character. Preachers are often unaware of this and unprepared to deal with the cultural and sub-cultural differences between and within different congregations. Pope Benedict's warning against 'generic and abstract homilies' included an emphasis upon the needs of the community, asking ministers 'to preach in such a way that the homily closely relates the proclamation of the word of God to the sacramental celebration *and the life of the community*, so that the word of God truly becomes the Church's vital nourishment and support.'[23]

American homileticist Leonora Tibbs Tisdale identifies three common faults among preachers: that of preparing 'generic sermons for generic humanity'; attributing 'attitudes, beliefs and values' to the congregation or projecting onto the congregation the preacher's own 'issues and concerns'.[24] It may be that the content of the message is clear to the preacher but the readiness of the congregation to hear it is another matter. For this reason it is important to try to establish an imaginative empathy with the hearers of the message, akin to the covenantal approach whereby the preacher, like the God of Israel in the Exodus, not only challenges, but also travels with and alongside the people on their pilgrimage to the Promised Land.

Exegesis of the Congregation

This approach reflects the renewed understanding of the Church as the pilgrim people of God.[25] Moreover the approach is not a new one. In the sixth century Gregory the Great in his Book of Pastoral Rule, III 1-3, catalogues the differences to be identified among those who hear the preacher. These include gender, economic and social status, personal temperament and psychological disposition, moral character, spiritual and bodily health, sexual experience and marital status. Gregory goes on to suggest different approaches to be adopted towards each of these categories of people in his congregation.

There may be some occasions when the preacher is able to operate within some common categories. For example, he might be preaching exclusively to elderly religious sisters of Irish background, to a guild of Catholic businessmen, or young offenders attending Mass in a penal institution. Members of these congregations would share much in common outlook and experience. However even in such unusually homogeneous groups there would still be people with different outlooks and needs. In the case of the normal Sunday Mass congregation in a parish the degree of diversity would be much wider – often varying even between those attending different masses in the same church on the same weekend.

It is probably not practicable or desirable to make a complete sociological survey and psychological profile of every congregation. However a broad checklist of questions for the preacher to ask could be useful. Such a list might follow some of Gregory's classification. A break-down by age and gender, educational level, social class, political and religious outlook, regularity of attendance and degree of personal religious commitment could all be usefully included. The visiting or occasional preacher will benefit from enquiring about such variables in the congregation. A priest or deacon involved with members of the congregation on a day-to-day basis will often have internalised this information from experience. There may be also events taking place at parish or at local, diocesan or national level: the death of a much-loved pastor, a public scandal in the life of the church, mass redundancies and unemployment in a local workplace or the calling of a national election. More positively, the preacher might decide to refer to a local act of heroism, the canonisation of a saint or the achievement of children in the parish school.

Inductive preaching requires a clear idea of who the preacher's hearers are and of their religious, social and ideological background. Often this will require the recognition that preachers do not always have exactly the same background or outlook as their congregations. Tisdale suggests: 'One way to bridge the gap is to view preaching as an act of constructing local theology.' She argues that the community is the author of contextual theology. Thus, 'preachers are local theologians, called to craft theology that is shaped for very particular communities of faith.'[26]

However contextual theology will be valid only if it is open to the wider local and global context. Issues of world news and of the universal church can never be far from the mind of any preacher or congregation, wheresoever situated. This is partly because human beings live increasingly in a 'global village' in which regional issues have world-wide significance. It is not only preachers who need to open up to their local congregations but local congregations to the world. The cultural and religious realities of the preacher and of the congregation will influence the way the text is mediated and interpreted.

Feedback Time

Comments to the preacher at the door of the Church may sometimes be instructive but also unrepresentative. In some black, mainly pentecostal churches worshippers sometimes call out 'Yes! Yes!', 'Amen' or 'Praise the Lord!' by way of affirmation of the preacher's message. Some even call out 'Help him, Lord!' – indicating that they are not happy with the sermon! A less spontaneous method of getting feedback is the 'partners in preaching' approach. Reuel L. Howe proposes a faith-sharing opportunity for members of the congregation to enable the preacher to provide an opportunity for the hearers to articulate a response to the Word of God and thus for the church to be strengthened by the sharing of faith by its members.[27] This approach converges with the understanding that all the baptised share in the priesthood of Christ and that all are called to hear the Gospel, live it out in their lives, and share in its proclamation. In this way it is hoped that the preacher will be affirmed and encouraged to continue the discipline of effective preaching. The group meets after the service. A facilitator chairs the discussion and ensures that each one of the members of the group has an equal opportunity to contribute so that no one individual dominates, and that the discussion also does not go beyond thirty minutes. Usually it is not recommended that the preacher should be present for the discussion, which is audio-recorded. The standard three questions asked by a facilitator are: 'How did God's Word and the homily touch your life today?', 'What difference will God's Word and the homily make in your week?' and 'Are the ways in which today's preacher might have improved in communicating the message?'

God's presence in the lives of his people

Such feedback strategies combine with the preacher's prior knowledge of the congregation so that the homily will be able to voice the congregation's concerns 'by naming its demons'[28], pointing 'to the signs of God's presence in the lives of his people'.[29] Within the framework of this approach, the preacher will forge a homily that reflects his own ethos but which also speaks to the way that his congregation and its society experience the world. Sometimes he will lead on from that experience to expand the horizons of his hearers to embrace a wider vision. When he does this however he will need to be particularly careful not to leave his congregation behind, never forgetting that it is just as important to ask 'Who am I preaching to?' as it is to ask '*What* is it that I am trying to preach?'

Preaching application: 'Inequitable lives'

To illustrate this approach I am including a homily that was prepared against the background of the

Equitable Life Pension failure of July 2004. The largely middle class congregation in a suburban London parish would have included a number of people worried about their retirement. The Gospel for the Nineteenth Sunday in Ordinary Time (Year B) was Luke 12:13-21 and the central message was seen to be that true security can be found only with the God who requires open handed generosity towards the poor. This insight was confirmed by reading David Buttrick's sermon on the Rich Farmer: 'The farmer was a fool: he tried to secure his own life. But he could have been rich towards God, serving God's friends, the poor.'[30]

Text of the Homily

My experience as a preacher tells me that if I start by asking whether you have made adequate personal pension plans you will probably spend the next ten minutes thinking about that and miss the message of the rest of the homily! So I won't! But if I did, and you did then spend the next ten minutes thinking about your pensions, I wouldn't altogether blame you! We all know that people have been let down badly by mismanagement of pension schemes recently. Financial security is not to be sniffed at even if other things are even more important. We all need some sense of security.

Calling the rich man a fool seems problematic

So why does God tell the rich man he was a fool? He started by thinking about financial security in his old age and never got round to thinking about anything else. That he was 'not rich before God' is often understood to mean that he did not share his bumper harvest with the poor. Bumper harvests were meant to

37

be a bonanza for everyone not just for the farmers. Almsgiving is what makes someone rich with God. We might sympathise with the rich fool. He just minded his own business and minded it rather well. He made prudent provision for the future. He didn't know he was about to die. It is just a fact of life that big questions can be a big distraction, distracting us from giving time to thinking either about our relationship with God or of our responsibilities to the poor. The rich fool was no more of a fool than most. But in the parable God says 'Fool, this night your soul is required of you.'

Jesus reminds us of our real situation

It may help if we look at what prompted the parable. Jesus was on his way to Jerusalem to die. He was in the middle of teaching that those who wished to be his disciples would need to be ready to face opposition and even death. But they aren't all listening. A man in the crowd ignores what Jesus is saying and asks him to rule on a property dispute. We don't know whether the man was in the right in the dispute or not. The point is that he was not paying attention to the big question about being rich before God.

A counter-cultural message

When we apply this message to our time we can see that this parable has never been more topical. The privileged classes in developed countries enjoy a higher standard of living than ever. We are constantly encouraged to consume beyond any possible need. While the earth's resources are squandered, millions of people in the poorer countries are deprived of basic necessities: food, clean water, health and education.

Even in developed countries disparities between the rich and the poor are astonishing. In today's world individual almsgiving can help but it cannot resolve these problems. Over production and over consumption are apparently required if the economy is to flourish. They are built into the very structure of our society. If they are to be changed we must mobilise public opinion for change and that will require a revolution in attitudes and expectations. A fool in the Bible is someone who is an atheist: 'The fool has said in his heart there is no God' (Psalm 14:1). And people who say that they believe in God can act as though they did not, just as people who say that they don't believe sometimes behave as though they did. If we ignore all the injustice and poverty in our world then we act like atheists, concerned only with saving up for those luxury cruises in our old age. Without our savings and our pensions we fear that we cannot be secure about getting in on the party. And God says 'Fool, this night your soul is required of you.'

If we think like that then we are fools before God, rejecting the only real security on offer: the security of having been brought back to life in Christ. It is being brought back to life in Christ that we celebrate in the Eucharist. It is in the Eucharist that we find the strength to go up to Jerusalem with Jesus and to share in his insecurity.

***

CHAPTER 3

'Interpreting the Text': Proclaiming the Word

Preaching Application: Trinity Homilies

'The gift of speech which you have granted to me can have no greater reward than to serve you by preaching you and showing you for what you are, as Father, Father indeed of the only begotten God...'

(St Hilary on the Trinity,[31])

The content of our preaching is the Living God who is revealed in the incarnation, life, death and resurrection of Christ. In the scripture readings, explained in the homily, God is speaking to his people 'opening up to them the mystery of redemption and salvation, and nourishing their spirit' and 'Christ himself is present in the midst of the faithful through his word'.[32]

The preacher of the homily always stands under this Word, submitting what he says to the authority of the Word of God in the Scriptures. Like the Word of God in Tradition, Scripture mirrors and expresses Jesus Christ, the living Word; the second Person of the Holy Trinity. Thus, all preaching should be Trinitarian. This does not mean that the preacher should be continually expounding the doctrine of the Trinity. Rather it is the reality of the Trinity that is revealed in his preaching, a reality which must always structure the presentation of the message. The Good News we preach is that God the Father is revealed to us through the incarnation of his Son, that he reconciles us to himself through Christ's death and resurrection and that his Holy Spirit is now poured out into our hearts (for example: John 1:1-14, Timothy 1:14, Titus 2:13, 3:8 and Hebrews 1:1-4). This is the message of every sound homily ever preached. The task of the preacher is to see this message as refracted through the texts and the season of each liturgy, to help it to come alive in the minds and the imagination of his congregation and to relate it to their lives and to the times in which they live.

The developed doctrine of the Trinity is not clearly stated in the Bible. However, Old Testament images and types foreshadow it and in the New Testament it is implicit in the words that are used about Jesus and about the Spirit. Jesus addresses God as his Father, speaks about the Father and presents himself as the way to the Father. He also offers the promise of the Spirit who will place the disciples in a new relationship with the Father. This new relationship with the Father derives from being sisters and brothers with Jesus and sharing in the common spirit as daughters and as sons. This theme runs through the epistles of Paul and in the sermons of Peter in the Acts of the Apostles (Acts 2:14-36, 3:11-26 and 10:36-43). The preacher is a proclaimer of this living message of the new relationship with God in Christ before he is a communicator of information. He has a different role from that of either the theologian or the lecturer in Biblical Studies.

Theology provides an analytic approach to the theory and practice of Christian Faith and this includes dogmatic formulations and authentic church teaching. Respectively, these provide foundations and guidelines for theologians, but theological investigation is, of its nature, often tentative and its conclusions provisional.

Preaching, on the other hand, involves the presentation of a message confident enough to seek to turn the 'world upside down' (Acts 17:16). Similarly, Biblical Studies are concerned with the exploration of the Scriptures in their own integrity as well as in the tradition of the Church. This task involves critical scrutiny of the texts in the light of the available evidence including archaeology, philology, and comparative contemporary literature as well as insights derived from the study of sources and of the processes of redaction. By contrast, the preacher is not so much concerned with explaining these texts as with interpreting the human situation in the light of them. This demands that he should 'get behind' these texts as 'real words addressed to real people'.[33]

The Bread of the Word and the Bread of the Eucharist

The homily is an integral part of the liturgy, applying the meaning of one or all of the appointed readings in the Liturgy of the Word so as to proclaim the presence of Christ in the lives of the congregation and the world in which they live. Christ is present in the Word of Scripture and the homily 'must always lead the community of the faithful to celebrate the Eucharist wholeheartedly so that they may hold fast in their lives to what they have grasped by their faith'.[34] Thus, 'there is an integral ritual relationship between what is proclaimed and heard in the Liturgy of the Word and the Liturgy of the Eucharist that follows'.[35] The sharing in the bread of the Word should enable the people to prepare to share more fully in the bread of the Eucharist.

It is this liturgical context which differentiates a homily from a sermon. A 'sermon' usually refers to a 'free-standing' preaching that develops a text or theme not rooted in the scripture readings or liturgical texts that make up the service. Prior to the reforms of the second Vatican Council the preaching at a Sunday Mass could properly be described as a sermon since it was frequently quite unrelated to the readings.[36] A sermon may be lengthier than a homily and may often be the climax of a service of the Word. In some Protestant traditions this is the normal pattern of Sunday preaching and worship. Sermons also often take place in such contexts as a University Sermon or a lunchtime address. By contrast the homily is preached so that it 'flows from the liturgical action of which it is a part. It flows from the Scriptures...and it enables the congregation to participate in the celebration with faith'.[37]

The 'First Naïveté'

The first step in preparation for this process requires that the preacher should make the message his own through prayer and meditation on the text to a point where he can identify a central message in one clear sentence – one central idea around which the homily can be built. This primary intuition – what Paul Ricœur calls the 'first naïveté' – will then need to be reassessed in the light of historical-critical understanding. *Fulfilled in your hearing* urges that 'there is nothing more essential than prayerful listening for effective preaching'[38] and suggests a whole week of daily meditation on the Sunday texts alongside the serious study of scholarly commentary.

The historical-critical method

Such study is essential if the preacher is to be an effective 'mediator of meaning'. He needs to understand the peoples and times of the biblical texts, to appreciate their significance both to those who wrote them and to those who first heard them read as well as the processes by which texts were recorded, transmitted, edited and understood. The Biblical Commission holds up the historical-critical method as 'an indispensable method for the scientific study of the meaning of ancient texts…reminding us that the Bible is the word of God in human language', having human authors as well as a Divine author. Because of this, we are told, 'its proper understanding not only admits the use of this method but also actually requires it' as providing 'fresh access to the Bible…' It further argues that pre-modern Jewish or Christian interpretation of the Bible had no clear awareness of the concrete and diverse historical conditions in which the word of God took root among the people; of all this it had only a general and remote awareness.[39]

Preachers who are not biblical scholars will need to rely upon secondary sources such as good commentaries in order to access and use the contributions of historical critical scholarship. The American Bishops suggest that interpretation of the Bible requires the best use of available biblical scholarship depending on the personal resources of the preacher, who will need to build up a basic library of scholarly commentaries. Also, since the preacher is not proclaiming his own message, he needs to be firmly rooted in the doctrine of the Church 'nourished by profound meditation upon the inspired Word, the exegesis of the fathers, conciliar documents and the teaching of the magisterium'.[40]

The preacher needs to be open to what can be learned from critical approaches but he should not clutter his homily with unnecessary details. He must be aware that 'the presentation of the Gospels should be done in such a way as to elicit an encounter with Christ, who provides the key to the whole biblical revelation and communicates the call of God that summons each one to respond'. Moreover his message 'ought to appear as something addressed to Christians now...Good hermeneutical principles are necessary to attain this end. Want of preparation in this area leads to the temptation to avoid plumbing the depths of the biblical readings and to being content simply to moralise or to speak of contemporary issues in a way that fails to shed upon them the light of God's word.' Preachers are reminded that they should avoid insisting in a one-sided way on the obligations incumbent upon believers, focussing instead on the message as 'good news of salvation freely offered by God'.[41]

Within the framework of this approach, the preacher will forge an appropriate interpretative approach reflecting his own ethos and one that speaks to the way that his congregation and their society experience the world. Sometimes he will lead on from that experience to expand the horizons of his hearers to embrace a wider vision. When he does this however he will need to be particularly careful not to leave his congregation behind.

The power of the Word

If he is to understand and interpret the text of Scripture the preacher needs to have openness to its spiritual power, a grasp of critical biblical scholarship, knowledge of Tradition and the guidance of the Magisterium of the Church. Each of these elements will help to inform a sound approach to the homily. Alongside historical and textual criticism the preacher needs to consider the living tradition of the Church and the guidance provided by the magisterium – the teaching authority of the pope and the bishops.

Experience shows these aids to understanding and interpretation combine to unlock rather than to lock in the meaning of the text. There are as many different hermeneutics as there are interpreters or frameworks of interpretation. When each element is taken seriously, room remains for considerable freedom and diversity of approach, allowing the text to speak to the insights of the preacher and the congregation against the background of the culture and time in which they live.

Augustine pointed to the inter-connectiveness of Word and Sacrament, the verbal and the visible, when he calls the sacramental actions of liturgy the *'verbum visible'*, the Word made visible in the celebratory symbols, actions and gestures. This means that the message is always more than the exegesis of one or more portion of Scripture. It is always the Living God revealed in Christ that is preached; a message illuminated by the lectionary readings, but pointing beyond them to the Father of the only begotten God whose incarnation, death and resurrection are celebrated and sacramentally re-enacted in the Eucharistic celebration.

Preaching application:
A Homily for the Feast of the Holy Trinity

The aim of this sermon was to communicate that the Holy Trinity is not something we understand. It is something we experience. It is about our changed relationship with God and it changes our relationships with each other. Since the sermon given at a Word Service at Twickenham United Reformed Church, a reference to the Eucharist was not made. The readings used were those for Trinity Sunday in Year C: Isaiah 6:1-8; Psalm 29, Romans 8:12-17, John 3:1-17.

Text of the Sermon

Introduction: Celebrating a conundrum?

Some people are fascinated by puzzles. Husbands and wives sometimes have rows about who is going to do the quick crossword. People miss appointments because they get completely absorbed in a Sudoku.

There is a little known creed called the Athanasian Creed, and it includes these words: 'the Father is God, the Son is God and the Holy Spirit is God and yet there are not three gods but one God.' However true that is, it sounds like just words – and rather contradictory-sounding words at that…all it really tells us is that God is beyond our understanding.

Today is one of the few feasts that commemorate a doctrine rather than an event. Doctrines are useful because they draw boundaries. If we go beyond them we are no longer on home ground, we are no longer talking about the faith of the Church of Jesus Christ. But the one God, Father, Son and Holy Spirit, is not an intellectual conundrum. The Trinity is not intended to puzzle us but to give shape to our faith and our prayer. We are talking about the way our lives are changed by Jesus Christ.

The Good News of God's love and our response

The Gospel you have just heard is about that new life. Nicodemus, who came to talk to Jesus secretly by night, has just asked Jesus how someone can be born again – can experience new life. And the answer is that it is a gift. God has loved the world so much that he has given his only Son so that we may share in a life that is not only new but eternal. And with the gift goes a warning that whoever refuses to be believed is condemned. Notice, Jesus doesn't say whoever doesn't believe will be condemned. He says to refuse to believe is to be condemned already, 'because that person has refused to believe in the name of God's only Son'. Anyone who recognises that, 'God loved the world so much that he gave his only Son' and then refuses to accept it does not have to wait to the next life to be condemned. Their hardness of heart in the face of so much love and generosity means that they condemn themselves already. God's love is sheer gift and it comes to us through the good news about the death and resurrection of Jesus.

Application

In 2 Corinthians, Paul prays a trinitarian prayer that we often adapt and use in our worship: 'The grace of our Lord Jesus Christ, the love of God and the fellowship of the Holy Spirit be with *us* all.' By *grace* he means a new relationship with God that is utter gift – gift because we could never deserve it and because it comes from the overflowing love of the Father enabling us to share new life together in the Holy Spirit.

So when we ask what difference the Trinity makes to our lives we are not asking about a doctrine beyond our understanding, we are asking about how we experience the new life Jesus came to bring. The Holy Trinity changes our lives. The Holy Trinity should shape our relations with each other as Christians in different church traditions. The Holy Trinity should shape our prayer and our politics. The Holy Trinity is not something we understand but something we experience. It is about how we pray – through Jesus to the Father, in the power of the Spirit. Of course we can pray to Jesus and the Holy Spirit but the model of prayer in scripture and in the worship of the Church is usually to pray to God in the Holy Spirit through Jesus who is our brother, reconciling us to the Father and to each other. The Holy Trinity is about our changed relationship with God and with each other. It is about the way we live our lives. Paul tells us that the Holy Spirit we received in baptism is the power that makes us co-heirs with Christ, adopted as sons and daughters of God able to call him 'Father'. We are not here today just to celebrate a doctrine about a God who is beyond our telling – we are celebrating love and peace that is also beyond telling – eternal life in Jesus Christ.

CHAPTER 4

'Breaking the Word':
Linking Word and Sacrament

*'Another way of structuring the homily...is to
begin with a description of an interpretation or
reiteration of the text. After the human situation
has been addressed, the homilist can turn to the
Scriptures to interpret the situation, showing that
God is present and active in our lives today.'*

(*Fulfilled in Your Hearing*, 24)

Fulfilled in Your Hearing[42]

Among the many reasons why Catholics fall away,
many may never have heard the message of the Gospel
proclaimed clearly enough to persuade them that the
Church has anything to offer. The aim of preaching is
to involve the participants in what is heard and to call
forth the response of the hearer to the disclosure of
God's seeking love. In the liturgy the preacher has the
task of 'breaking the Word', making it digestible, so as
to communicate the 'good news' of Jesus Christ.

Linking Word and Sacrament

The Second Vatican Council spells out that when the
Scriptures are read in the Church, God himself is
speaking to his people. Christ is present in his own
word, proclaiming his good news. It is for this reason
that both the readings and the homily are seen as 'a
living commentary on the word'. As such they are
integral parts of the liturgical action.[43] Preaching is

seen not only a primary means of evangelisation but is integrally linked with the nourishment given in the Eucharist.[44] The proclamation of the Lord's death and resurrection in the Liturgy of the Word is inseparable from the self-offering of Christ in the Eucharist.[45] This close link between Word and Sacrament derives from the belief of the Church that Christ is present in the word that is proclaimed and preached. The essential meaning of the Word must be grasped, analysed and then connected to the 'Paschal Mystery' celebrated by the Church so that it can transform hearts and minds.

The 'new homiletic', pioneered by Protestant North American homileticians, offers a powerful vision for this transforming of hearts and minds. Tom Troeger urges that preachers 'need to build sermons so that our listeners can step securely from image to image, from story to story and thus climb into the truths of lives'.[46] Eugene Lowry argues that a sermon is an event that happens. Preaching is an 'event-in-time'. Therefore the members of the congregation need to hear the message in such a way that their thinking is changed so as to lead them to greater faith in Christ. The sermon should not be constructed like an essay, laying one building block upon another. Lowry does not accept the common preaching practice of announcing what is going to be said, and then saying it and then telling the congregation what has been said. A good storyteller never gives away the climax of a story like that. Lowry suggests a five part methodology for 'the sermon as preached' (oops, ugh, aha, whee, and yeah – or conflict, complication, sudden shift, good news, and unfold-ing).[47] Sermons, like stories should have plot, tension, climax, etcetera.

Such high drama is evident not only in good

preaching but also in the scriptures themselves and the stages in Lowry's plot are often there in the Gospel stories already. For example, in John 8, conflict begins with the adulterous woman being brought to Jesus. The plot tightens in complication as her accusers try to trick Jesus into opposing the Law of Moses. Then comes the sudden shift; 'Let the one among you who is guiltless be the first to throw a stone.' The good news follows as each of the accusers goes away and the woman is told that she is not condemned by Jesus. The application is that she should sin no more. According to the circumstances of the congregation and the times, the preacher can use a number of interpretative approaches. For example, the plot might engage with a current witch-hunt in the media to invite awareness of our common sinfulness. It could be used to convince the guilt-ridden that Jesus does indeed have power to forgive sins. It might even be used to address the oppression of women by pointing to the absence of the woman's male partner and Jesus' advocacy for women in a men's world.

When this drama is preached the conflict and complication sections may incorporate local, national or international circumstances. Since Lowry is in a liberal evangelical tradition, his preaching plots do not envisage preaching at a Eucharist. When preaching at Mass the Catholic preacher should always incorporate a liturgical application into the unfolding stage of the homily.

The Lectionary Context

An additional context to liturgical preaching is provided by the lectionary context. The preacher who understands the character and purpose of the lectionary will be able to take advantage both of its strengths and of its limitations. The strength of the lectionary consists in the help it offers the preacher in interpreting a text both in the light of the other prescribed biblical texts and in the light of the mind of the Church. The limitations of the lectionary have the useful function of turning the preacher's attention back to the Bible itself. So for example, the lectionary offers help to the preacher by providing a key to preaching a Gospel text as illuminated by an examination of the first and/or second readings. Thematically linked readings provide thematic links with the gospel passage, reinforcing the primary message of the Mass of the day. In such cases it may be possible to pass freely from one reading to another – for example finding conflicts and complications, good news and clues as to the application of the good news first in one reading and then in another. As we have seen the second reading is not always thematically linked but forms part of a continuous or semi-continuous reading. In such cases any relevance to the theme of the Mass is purely adventitious. This is also true of the first reading and the Gospel on weekdays in ordinary time. Occasionally, but rarely, it is possible to discern a common thread that was not evident to the compilers of the lectionary. Normally however, if the preacher decides to make use of unrelated texts in his preaching it will probably by way of one passing illustration, phrase or example. Again, it is important not to force a thematic unity between the second reading and the gospel reading where none exists.

The positioning of the text in relation to the other texts offers a perspective of interpretation according to the mind of the Church, which provides a key to interpreting the text relative to the place in the lectionary where it occurs and to the celebration it serves. One example of a text used more than once in the lectionary can illustrate this point. The Wedding Feast at Cana (John 2:1-11) is provided for the Second Sunday in Ordinary Time in Year C, for 7 January (in countries where the Epiphany is celebrated on a Sunday that falls on 8 January), as an option for the Gospel for the Common of the Blessed Virgin Mary, for the optional memorial for Our Lady of Lourdes on 11 February and, finally, as an option for use at the celebration of a marriage. In the first two instances the text would be read in the light of the theme of the feast of the Epiphany and the emphasis would lie on the character of the event as a manifestation of Christ allied with the other two Epiphany narratives: the Star of Bethlehem and the Baptism of the Lord. Preaching on the text in a Marian context would emphasise the actions and words of Mary at the wedding feast and the use of the story at a wedding could be expected to explore the relevance of the presence of Jesus at the marriage in Cana for the future life together of the couple being married at the wedding where the homily is preached.

The Scriptural Context

One of the limitations of the lectionary consists in its inability to provide the full context of each passage. So for example, sometimes a parable, a miracle or a group of sayings of Jesus are offered without any indication of what immediately precedes or follows them or of where they come from within the overall framework of the Gospel narrative. At other times one or more verses are left out entirely. Awareness of this limitation should send the preacher to the Bible to discover what meaning can be derived from the overall context. Thus, no preacher should ever preach on a gospel consisting of sayings of Jesus drawn from John 14:1 to 16:33 without explaining that these are words spoken by Jesus after the Last Supper, awaiting betrayal on the night before his crucifixion. Without this reference the significance and poignancy of Jesus' words cannot be fully appreciated or applied. The preacher has the freedom to base the homily on any of the readings appointed for the day, but it may be helpful to read and meditate on the first reading and try to discern the thematic link with the Gospel. It may also help to examine the passage in its original context, noting whatever events or other materials precedes and follow the passage. The same procedure can be followed with the responsorial psalm and with the second reading, remembering that the psalm is always intended to have a thematic link with the Gospel but that during in ordinary time the second reading does not have this link.

The final stages of preparation can usefully involve writing out the homily in full, fitting it into sections reflecting each of the 'moves'. It is helpful to conclude by going over the text again and again, both as a personal meditation and as rehearsal for the final preaching. The preacher may even decide to read the text into a recorder and listen to it over again to reflect and improve on delivery and sharpen the structure and wording of the message. Although use of a 'canned' or generic homily is always a mistake, other people's homilies may offer some useful angles once the preparation has reached its final stage.

Practical advice on preaching can be debated and argued over. There are as many ways of preaching as there are preachers, and good preaching technique is always subordinate to the overall aim of proclaiming the good news. A masterful performance may impress the congregation and, nevertheless, carry no conviction at all. Likewise a homily may impress everyone with the evident sincerity or learning of the preacher but leave each person wondering what point the preacher was trying to make. It is the good news about Jesus which is the 'splendour of preachers' and this good news needs to be proclaimed clearly to those who may have attended Mass for years without ever hearing it. With the help of God, the preacher has the task of developing eloquence, relying totally on the Holy Spirit and, at the same time, doing everything possible, as St Augustine advocates, to 'teach, delight and persuade', involving the congregation in what they hear and inviting a response to the disclosure of God's seeking love. Clearly this is a difficult and challenging task. We should remember that the homily is an instrument but that it is God who uses it. In the words of the Redemptorist priest, Jim McManus, preaching 'is not simply an exercise in human discourse. Preaching is the proclamation of the word of God in and through human discourse. In and through the word of the preacher, the word of God is spoken to the individual. And through hearing the word of God the community is called to conversion'.[48]

Preaching application:
Two Homilies for All Saints' Day

1. 'What would Jesus do?'

The first homily was given for the Upper School of a Roman Catholic Comprehensive school in a London suburb. All the pupils are expected to be present at this school Mass. Two thirds are Catholics but less than half of that number are practising. Of the remaining third, a few are practising members of other Christian churches and some are members of other faith communities.

Text of the Homily

The risen Jesus is revealed in his saints. We can become like them through his grace.

In parts of the USA, asking 'What would Jesus do?' is a popular way of trying to decide difficult questions. Some environmentally conscious Christians are asking what kind of car Jesus would have chosen! However, even to ask the question in that way stretches the imagination too far. Jesus never even saw a car. He knew nothing about mobile phones, i-pods or play stations either. He lived one life at one time. Like any other human being, the Jesus who lived on earth had a limited experience. He was a man and not a woman; a Jew and not a gentile. He was a first-century man who probably never travelled far from what is today Israel-Palestine. He was not married and had no children – so we assume he knew nothing about the story in the *Da Vinci Code*! He never knew what it was like to be forty. He never had the opportunity to grow old.

Long ago and far away

So since he lived long ago and far away, with a very limited range of human experience, we might think that his example is not much use for showing us how we live our lives today.

Sudden shift

But Jesus is risen from the dead and we can see him in his Body, the Church. We see him in his saints. So who are his saints and how did they get that way?

True Blessedness

They are the men and women who followed his teaching and became happy because they were 'poor in spirit'. That means that they knew that God's kingdom was a gift rather than something that God owed them because they were rich or important or because they were particularly good. They were gentle, which means that it was them, rather than the pushy aggressive types who inherited the Promised Land of heaven. They mourned; but they were sad for the right reasons – sad because of the unfairness in the world – and they were comforted by God. They were merciful and were rewarded by God's mercy for them. They were hungry and thirsty for justice. They were single minded about wanting to see God – that is what 'pure in heart' means – and they were satisfied. Their work for peace made them God's children. They were ready to put up with being bullied for what was right and to put up with all kinds of insults for being Christians. As a result, they are happy now with 'a reward that is great in heaven'.

The saints lived in every place and in every time. Only a tiny fraction of them were named as saints by the Church. Some of them may have been people we have known – some of our own friends and family even. They spoke different languages; they were different colours, belonged to different cultures and had different temperaments. They all had one thing in common: they did not rely on their own strength to become saints. They became saints because of the love the Father lavished upon them. They washed their robes white again in the blood of the Lamb and now they see God as he really is.

***

2. A Story for All Saints' Day

This homily was given for a congregation of children aged between five and eleven at an All Saints' Day Mass for a Roman Catholic primary school in a middle class London suburb. The approach is an example of child-centred narrative preaching.

Text of the Homily

Tricking and Treating

Patrick and Samantha had wanted to go out tricking and treating at Hallowe'en but their parents had said no. Dad said it was like begging and might frighten old people living alone. Mum thought that it would be dangerous to knock on the doors of people they didn't know. Patrick and Sam argued and were sent to bed early as a punishment.

Sam went to sleep but later she saw Patrick standing by her bed in his Harry Potter outfit. 'Come on,' he said. 'Let's go tricking and treating anyway.'

They slipped out the house without their parents knowing and went to a quiet road where nobody knew them.

At the first house a man came to the door. He was big, with a lot of white hair and bright eyes. 'Hello children!' he boomed, 'I'm Mister Angel and who are you?'

'I'm Samantha and this is my brother Patrick and we are tricking and treating.'

'What is that?' he asked. 'I don't understand.'

'The idea is that you give us something nice or we will play a trick on you,' explained Patrick. 'So you'd better give us something nice.'

'Come in and I'll give you some cakes and lemonade,' said Mister Angel.

'Better not. Our parents told us not to go into houses with people we don't know.'

'That's alright,' said Mr Angel. 'I'll telephone your parents to see if it's alright.'

Patrick and Samantha said he didn't need to ring their parents after all.

When they were sitting down having their lemonade and cake Mr Angel looked at them very closely and asked them what they thought would make them happy when they grew up. Patrick wanted to be a tough guy so that nobody would ever push him about or get in the way of what he wanted. Sam wanted to be a pop star so that she would be rich and everyone would think that she was really cool. Mr Angel suddenly became very cross, grabbed them both by the shoulders and started to shake them very roughly. 'You are both very silly children!' he shouted. 'Don't you know that tomorrow is All Saints' Day?'

True Happiness

Sam woke up to find that her mother was shaking her, telling her that it was All Saints' Day and they would be late for the school Mass. On the way to school she told Patrick about her dream and was astonished to find that he had had the same dream.

At the Mass the deacon read to them that Jesus had said that the really happy people were not the famous or the strong but the poor in spirit, people who were gentle, cared about those who were sad, and who worked for peace. Even the people who were bullied or put in prison for being followers of Jesus were the really happy ones – and the deacon told them that there were places in the world where people were still punished for being Christians. The saints were our friends in heaven who had found true happiness by following Jesus during their lives on earth and living in the way Jesus had told them. Patrick and Sam decided that they wanted to be happy like the saints.

***

SECTION 2
Preaching at the Margins

CHAPTER 5

'Preaching Rebirth':
Preaching at an Infant Baptism

Unlike preaching at the Sunday Liturgy where the message of the preacher is largely directed to regular worshippers, congregations at weddings, baptisms and funerals often have little or no Christian background or commitment. The two homilies given here were prepared for infant baptisms celebrated outside of Mass where the parents and godparents, family and friends had tenuous links with Catholic faith or practice. The first homily focuses primarily upon Scripture texts and the second is an example of mystagogical preaching, where the preaching focus provides a commentary on the rite of baptism itself.

The Code of Canon Law (Can. 868 §1) specifies that, except when there is danger of death, a child should be accepted for the sacrament of baptism only where the parents or guardians, or at least one of them, is Catholic and at least one of the parents gives their consent. In also requires that 'that there be a well-founded hope' that the child be brought up as a Catholic. In cases where such hope is 'truly lacking' the baptism should be deferred and the parents advised of the reason. Such refusals are rare however and most pastors are naturally reluctant to turn away potential practising Catholics or to cut off one of the last links that residually Christian families may have with the Church. Inevitably then, congregations attending the celebration of the sacrament of baptism for infants may include a range of people, from committed Catholics to non-Christians whose attendance is dictated purely by considerations of friendship or family ties. Thus preaching at such celebrations needs to be directed both at building up the faith and understanding of believers and also at offering a sympathetic and inclusive introduction to the basics of the Christian faith for the outsider.

The parents or the parents and godparents are often invited to attend a series of preparatory meetings on the responsibility to bring up the child in the Faith. Such meetings provide an opportunity to introduce or reintroduce some understanding of the meaning of the sacrament of baptism and of the basics of the Christian Faith. The preaching that accompanies the celebration itself can then build on such preparation but also needs to take account of the varying needs of the congregation as a whole, combining a primary intention of helping the parents and godparents to see the relevance of the sacrament and at the same time to attract others to the Christian faith in an inductive and inclusive way. Special concern is needed to emphasise that baptism is more than a 'naming ceremony' and that the baptism of a baby, unable to give its own consent, makes sense only in the context of subsequent Christian formation.

EXEGESIS OF THOSE ATTENDING THE CELEBRATIONS OF INFANT BAPTISM

The preaching for both the celebrations of baptism recounted here was for children of parents with tenuous Church links. (Although based on actual baptisms, the names and the pastoral details have been changed.)

The first baby, Tom, already two years old, had a father who attended mass only at Christmas and Easter – and not always then! The mother, herself unbaptised, had no links with any Christian Church. Motives for bringing the child for baptism were not clear but may have included a desire to please the father's parents and by the excellent reputation of the local Catholic Primary School. More positively, Tom's parents, who were not canonically married, both expressed a concern for passing on sound spiritual and moral values and Tom's father related these to his own sense of identity as a Catholic. He also expressed a commitment to bringing the child to Church regularly at some stage in the future. The second child, Caitlin, had an intermittently practicing single mother who was very emotionally dependent on her own mother, a devout and very traditional Irish Catholic whose husband had died some years before. The twenty or so 'guests' at the baptisms of Tom and Caitlin were largely composed of lapsed Catholics, nominal Anglicans and non-believers.

Choice of Readings

The Gospel reading for Tom's baptism was taken from John's Gospel, 3:1-8, the meeting with Nicodemus and that for Caitlin from Mark, 10:13-16 where Jesus asks that the little children should be brought to him.

Interpretive Technique

The philosopher Paul Ricoeur, a French philosopher who taught at the University of Chicago, offers a 'hermeneutic of suspicion' in an approach to any text. This involves openness to a primary insight as to the meaning of a text which he terms the 'first naïveté.' A second stage in Ricoeur's pattern assumes critical distance and combines with the first naïveté to provide an interpretation of 'critical openness'.[49]

When applied to the interpretation of John 3:1-8, Ricoeur's method of interpretation produced a first naïveté that the child was being brought to a new birth by water and the Holy Spirit. The second naïveté, deepening the first, developed from reading commentaries on John's Gospel. In the Jerusalem Bible, John 3:4 is translated as 'I tell you most solemnly, unless a man is born from above he cannot see the kingdom of God'. According to Raymond Brown,[50] the Greek words *gennethe anothen*, translated 'born from above', have the double meaning of 'born from above' or 'born again'. Brown call this the 'technique of misunderstanding' whereby the confusion enables John to correct Nicodemus' somewhat prosaic interpretation of the words of Jesus as meaning that the birth must take place 'again in time'. 'Nicodemus' use of *deuteron*, as in 'Can he go back into the womb and be born *again*?', 'indicates that he chooses only the temporal meaning of *anothen*'.[51] Meanwhile a social science perspective emphasises that whatever status attached to a child's birth 'was simply a given. It usually stayed with a person for life… aside from extraordinary circumstances; a non-elite peasant remained a non-elite peasant until death. To be born *over again*, born for the second time…, would alter one's ascribed honour-status in a very fundamental way. A new honour-ascribed status would derive from a new birth'.[52]

These critical insights were incorporated into the development of an inductive preaching strategy for the infant Tom's baptism. By playing with images and reminders of Tom's birth and the emotions it had produced at the time, the homily could work on the idea of what a second birth might mean. Just as Tom had a special place in the world through his birth into his particular family and the gifts he had received through them, so now he would be born into a new family as a child of God, born again in the Spirit into a new life in Christ. This gift of new birth would require help and encouragement from his parents and god-parents who might need to be reminded of what a wonderful gift it really is.

Text of the Homily for Tom's Baptism

'Just for a moment I would like you to think about how you felt when Tom was born: relief that mother and baby were alright; wonder that such an amazing thing as the birth of a new human being could happen to you and, above all, just sheer joy at the birth of a new member of the human family. And Tom didn't just become part of the human family in general; he became part of a particular family with his parents, his grandparents and other relations. That is why so many of them are here today, together with their friends.

So today is a great family occasion; but it is not only that. It is not just a naming ceremony. Tom has had his name since he was born. No, today is about Tom becoming a member of another family – the family of the Church. Through the power of God's Holy Spirit Tom will become a brother of Jesus Christ and a child of God the Father. He will be 'born again'; 'born from above'. Nicodemus, the man who came to visit Jesus at night couldn't get his head round that. He said 'How can a grown man be born? Can he go back into his mother's womb and be born again?' Not even someone as young as Tom can do that! So what was Jesus talking about?

You may have heard of people who call themselves 'born again Christians'. Actually there isn't any other kind! As far as the Catholic Church is concerned every baptised Christian is 'born again' – it is just that in many cases they are not born again so that you would notice! They either do not believe that Jesus died on the cross and rose again so as to give them a wonderful new life or else they believe it and don't really care. But Jesus is the giver of this gift of being born again – of being able to start a new life as his brother and as a child of the Father – and the gift is real.

Imagine that a particularly generous friend of Tom's parents gives Tom a very special 'state of the art' laptop computer. Then imagine that it never gets taken out of the box. Nobody ever encourages Tom to play with it or offers to teach him how to use it. The gift will be real enough but it will not be much use to him! That is why Tom's parents and godparents will have such an important role to play in helping him to grow in the new life that Christ gives him. This new life will bring him even greater happiness than any other gift he could ever receive and unlike any other gift it will last for ever!

[Several elements in this short homily were then underlined further with a selection of brief commentaries on the ceremonies accompanying the rite itself as in the section that follows.]

***

Mystagogical preaching for the Baptism of Caitlin

The word mystagogy is taken from the Greek *Mystagogia,* meaning 'interpreting of mystery' (literally, 'the leading of the initiated'). In the early centuries of the Church, it came to be used in a specifically Christian way, referring to the stages of Christian initiation, through which new adult Christians were led to a deeper understanding of their Baptism, Confirmation and first Holy Communion at Easter. The term 'mystagogical preaching' can be used to refer to any preaching that invites the initiated Christian to reflect on the deeper meaning of their sacramental experience. In the case of the celebration of baptism for an infant I am suggesting the preaching of a brief running commentary on the various stages of the rite in order to awaken in the parents and godparents a sense of the significance of their own baptism so as to encourage them to help the child to grow in the Faith.

Although the preaching at Caitlin's baptism chiefly consisted of commentary on the rite itself, a brief treatment of the Gospel reading from Mark 10:13-16 was also required. Although this text relates only indirectly to infant baptism, it was used very early on to justify the baptism of infants. One commentary argues that 'there is no reason to read this idea back into Mark' at the same time allowing that 'it may have resonated with some in the Markan community'.[53] More positively Oscar Cullmann rejected also the idea that any debate over infant baptism was foreseen by Jesus or that 'the primitive church invented the occurrence of Mark 10:13-16 to justify infant baptism'. Instead he suggested that the story was included into the narrative in 'such a way that a baptismal formula of the first century gleams through it'.[54] This insight renders the account of the incident a particularly valuable text to include within a mystagogical preaching commentary on the ceremony as a whole.

Text of the Homily for Caitlin's Baptism

At the reception of the child at the Church door the priest or deacon asks the parents what they ask from God's Church and what name they intend to give to the child. He then reminds the parents and godparents of their duties and invites them to follow him in making the sign of the cross on the child's forehead:

'I expect that this baby has already received some gifts from her mother's friends and family. Some people may even have asked what to give. On behalf of the Church I am now going to ask you what you want as a gift from the Church. So, I now ask you, *What do you ask of the Church?*

A name tells us who we are and the name you are going to give this child will be her baptism name, the name she will have as a child of God. *So what name do you give this child?*

Adults will make lots of decisions for Caitlin before she is old enough to make them for herself. They will decide that she needs to have regular food and drink, to be kept clean and, as she grows, to be sensitive to others. The most important decision anyone will make for her is that she is to be a child of God and a sister of Jesus Christ, filled with his Holy Spirit. This gift of being a child of God must not be like a wrapped up present left under the Christmas tree. She will need help in opening it up and finding out how to make it work properly. So I will now ask her mother and her godparents to make a solemn statement that they understand what they are undertaking.

You have asked for your child to be baptised…
Do you clearly understand what you are undertaking?
Are you ready to help Caitlin's mother in her duty as a Christian mother?

I am now going to read from Mark's Gospel 10:13-16.

Now that we have heard this story let us think about what it means. People were bringing their children to Jesus just as you have brought Caitlin today. But there was a problem. The disciples of Jesus thought that it wasn't appropriate. Jesus had a message for grown ups and they probably thought that bringing children to him was wasting his time. There are some Christians today who will baptise only people old enough to understand. Maybe some people thought like that at the time that Mark's Gospel was written and that was why Mark decided to put this incident from the life of Jesus in his Gospel – to show that children as well as adults could share the new life that Jesus gained for us when he died for us and rose again.

The disciples had tried to keep the children away but Jesus was indignant and told them to let the little children come to him and not to stop them. And he said that only people who grow in simple trust like young children would be able to come into his kingdom. The promises you have just made will help this child to come to Jesus, not just today, but when she come to make her first Holy Communion and when she is confirmed. With the help of your prayers and example she will be blessed and embraced by Jesus all through her life until she comes to the end of her time on earth and comes to share in the kingdom that God has prepared for those who love him.

So now we are going to pray for this child, her parents and her godparents and after each prayer I would like you to say 'Lord Hear Our Prayer'.

– (*At the end of first set of the intercessions*) 'In a minute Caitlin is going to become part of a Church that has members in heaven as well as on earth so we are going to ask their prayers and we say, "Pray for us" after each petition.'

– (*Before the prayer of exorcism*) 'We have only to watch the news to see that the human race is caught up in a lot of evil that is not always entirely the fault of the individuals concerned. Sometimes we hear someone blaming the parents. Then we look at the parents and we are tempted to blame their parents or perhaps we blame advertising, the culture or the media. What is clear is that nobody gets a fair start. We are already part of a web of human evil from the very beginning. So now I am going to tell Satan, the spirit of evil, to leave this child alone, because she is going to become part of a network of love and goodness through the presence of the Holy Spirit in her life.'

– (*Before the prayer of anointing*) 'Before she is baptised we remind ourselves that she is to be like an athlete who has had ointment rubbed on her muscles to make her ready for an athletic event. So I will now anoint her with oil to represent the strength she will need to be a disciple of Christ.'

– *(Before the blessing of the water)* 'None of us can live without water. The Bible begins by reminding us that water covered the earth before dry land appeared. The story of Noah reminds us that water can destroy us. The story of the Israelites escaping from the Egyptians through the Red Sea reminds us that God can put clear water between us and whatever threatens us. John baptised Jesus in the river Jordan. Water flowed from the side of Christ on the cross and Jesus told his disciples to baptise all nations in the name of the Father and of the Son and of the Holy Spirit. Water is the symbol of new life and I am now going to bless this water so that Caitlin will share in the life of the risen Jesus.'

— (*Before the renunciation of sin, the profession of faith and the baptism*) 'Living this new life means a turning away from sin – everything that is not filled with God's love. I am now going to ask Caitlin's mother and the godparents to renounce sin and to profess the faith on Caitlin's behalf. This is also an opportunity for them and for everyone here to renew their faith and to reaffirm the promises made on their behalf when they were baptised.'

— (*Before the baptism*) 'And now we come to the baptism itself. When I say "I baptise you", it will be Jesus Christ himself – not me – who is making this child part of the new creation brought about by his death on the cross and his resurrection from the dead.'

— (*Before the anointing after baptism*) 'I am now about to mark this child with the oil of chrism, blessed by the bishop. Anointing with oil is a very ancient way of marking somebody out as a leader, set apart for a special purpose. Christ is a priest, a prophet and a king and now that Caitlin shares in Christ's life she is set apart as a royal priest and a prophet like him.'

— (*Before the presentation of a candle and a white garment*) 'This new life is now going to be represented by a white garment symbolising the innocence of this new child of God. After that I will light a candle from the Easter Candle to symbolise that this child has been given the light of faith to light up the way she will live.'

– (*Concluding rites*) 'Jesus once touched the mouth and ears of a deaf and dumb person. He then said the word, '*Ephetha*', ('be opened' in Aramaic). Caitlin cannot speak or hear about the things of God yet. I will now perform a ceremony that reminds us that Caitlin will need all our help if the wonderful gift that she has received today is to have its full effect in her life. Then, before the final blessing we will join in the family prayer that Jesus taught to his disciples… "Our Father…"'

***

CHAPTER 6

'Preaching at Cana':
Preaching at Weddings

The proclamation and preaching of the Word in the context of the liturgy is a message primarily directed to building up the faith of those who are present in Church and who are united by a common faith and baptism. The guests at a wedding celebration are present from motives of friendship or family solidarity rather than out of shared religious faith. Frequently the congregation will include not only practising Catholics and other believing Christians, but an assortment of lapsed and semi-lapsed Catholics, residual Christians, people of other faiths, atheists, agnostics, and post-Christians: the unchurched and the semi-churched. In this case the wedding homily will need to respond to the challenge of adapting the Gospel message to the understanding and needs of people with very varying levels of faith commitment or theological under-standing. The opportunities for evangelisation present-ed by at such weddings are important but need to be approached with care. Firstly, because the primary purpose of a wedding homily is to address the two people getting married. Secondly, preaching on these occasions should be inclusive in its tone, making outsiders feel that they are privileged to be present to share in an event that celebrates the presence of God in all human lives, but which gains greater depth and meaning when linked with the mystery of Christ and the life of the Church.

In both the weddings described here the homily was intended to help couples getting married to see the relevance of Christ to their marriage and also to attract members of the congregation to the Christian faith and to a Christian understanding of marriage – and to do so in an inductive and inclusive way. The risk involved in this was that those in the congregation who were not practising Christians or whose life-style or relationships fell short of Christian ideals might feel alienated from the message. In each case preparation of the homily involved not only reflection on the chosen scripture texts but also upon the background of each of the couples and their guests. Each homily illustrates the application of distinct preaching approaches. Both were preached at actual weddings although the names of the brides and bridegrooms and their friends have been changed.

The happy couples and their guests

Both couples were in their mid thirties. David and Kathleen were both professionals in their late thirties. Kathleen was a practicing and committed Catholic, recently confirmed after a decade or more of inter-mittent attendance at Mass. David was brought up in the Society of Friends but no longer believes in God. David and Kathleen knew each other as young children and met again at a party three years before their wedding. Both are graduates who had also studied at post-graduate level.

Andrew is an on-line salesman with theologically-informed, practising Catholic parents of generally liberal religious opinions. Andrew was very intermit-tently practising and had resisted any attempt on his parents' part to explain even basic theological concepts.

Nevertheless he clearly had a Christian and Catholic identity. Lucy, an art teacher who also paints and exhibits her work, was a non-practising, baptised, Anglican with very little theological background ('I wasn't baptised, but I was christened.')

The congregation at both wedding services probably included more pagans than St Paul ever had the opportunity to preach to at any one time! Of the young people who made up three-quarters of both the large congregations probably only a few had ever been practising Christians of any stamp and a mere handful practiced as church members, even on an intermittent basis. Many of the younger guests were cohabiting with their partners, mostly with no intention of getting married, and several of the family guests were divorced and remarried. The congregation at Kathleen and David's wedding included a higher proportion of university-educated young people, most of whom could fairly be described as agnostic or atheist in their religious opinions.

The Scripture Readings

The first two readings, chosen by both couples, were the same (Song of Songs 2:8-10, 14, 16 and 8:6-7 and 1 Corinthians 12.31–13.8). Consultation with each of the two couples and with others planning the service led to a lively discussion as to the relevance and meaning of the texts chosen. The first reading: Song of Solomon 2:8-14 and 8:6-7 was chosen by both couples and affirmed by the others present because it reads as a beautiful Old Testament love poem. It needed to be explained that it has also been understood not just as a poem in praise of sexual and romantic love but as a symbol of the love of God for his people as well as for each and every individual in his world. The second reading, 1 Corinthians 12:31–13:8, was chosen because it was well known and popular. It was explained that St Paul is here describing the quality of real love, understood by Christians as the greatest virtue.

The Song of Songs is a celebration of the love between a shepherd and a shepherdess who each praise each other's beauty and proclaim in dramatic form their love and passion. It is doubtful whether either of the two couples who chose this reading was aware of the later mystical allegorical interpretations of the text. The choice of the verses from the Song of Songs was certainly based upon their beauty and the fact that they echo familiar human emotions of sexual and romantic love. The first two verses (2:8-10, 14 and 16) celebrate a surprise visit by the bridegroom. The bride hears his steps and likens his approach to that of stag speeding across the hillside. The bridegroom's invitation to his allegedly shy bride leads to a profession of the loving union between them; 'My beloved is mine and I am his.' The next extract from the Song (8:6-7) is probably spoken by the bridegroom who asks that the union between them should be like the signet ring attached to a string over the heart or tied to the arm. Their love is to be as inexorable as death and, just as Sheol never gives back the dead, so their love can never suffer alteration but will be like a fierce blaze that water cannot extinguish.

The second reading continues the theme of love but focuses on *agape* rather than *eros*. In ancient Greek texts *agape* can refer to brotherly love, the love between husband and wife or love for children but in the New Testament it appears as the quality of unconditional, indiscriminate love that is the necessary precondition for all genuine love. Here, in Paul, it is the basis for good works and, without it, charismatic gifts, religious faith, almsgiving and even self sacrifice would be meaningless (13:1-3). It exhibits qualities of tolerance and forbearance and is inconsistent with jealousy, boastfulness or arrogance (13:4-7).

Preparation Process of Preaching for David and Kathleen's wedding: 'Remain in My Love'

The Gospel passage for the wedding of Kathleen and David was John 15:9-12 ('Remain in my love'), chosen by the couple because it referred to love that would last. The fact that these verses form part of the farewell discourse of Jesus on the night before his trial and crucifixion gives a special poignancy to his proclamation of the love between the Father and the Son as the model and the source for the love that is to unite the disciples of Jesus. However, like the love of Jesus for his Father, the love of the disciples is to be validated by obedience to the law of love: 'to repeat in their relationship with Jesus, what Jesus has always had with the Father: a loving mutuality shown by the uncon- ditional observance of his commandments' (Maloney, 422).

The homily for Kathleen and David set out to communicate the insight that authentic and commit- ted human love is an experience of the transcendent love exemplified by the self giving of Jesus Christ. The homily plan used was based on Eugene Lowry's approach as outlined in his *The Homiletical Plot*, moving through the five parts methodology of conflict, complication, sudden shift, good news, and unfolding, giving examples and analogies.

The conflict and complication elements in the

homily for Kathleen and David's wedding turned around the questions of why the couple had decided to marry in Church and whether they were not, after all, celebrating little more than a biological attraction. The sudden shift turned on the contrast between a purely biological and reductive account of love between a man and a woman and the sublime language of the verses from the Song of Songs. However, whereas the Song of Songs was originally probably a hymn to romantic-erotic love, the passage from Corinthians brought the focus to bear upon *agape*, the selfless disinterested love that is at the centre of the Good News exemplified by Jesus in his words to the disciples on the night he was betrayed. The application of the good news consisted in a brief recommendation to the couple to see the mutual love that Jesus preached to his disciples as the model for their love for each other.

Text of the homily for Kathleen and David's wedding

Introduction: I have been told that this is an above average intellectual congregation, so I am pitching my remarks accordingly!

Conflict: The question I would like to address is why we are here. I know we are here out of affection for Kathleen and David, to share their joy and to wish them well – but we could be doing that in a registry office. Assuming they had the licence, they could even have been married beside a waterfall, in a private room in a pub or outside the small mammal house in the zoo. They might even have exchanged their vows while bungee-jumping, saying 'I do' as they passed the minister on the way up and down. We might be here, in this particular church because, as I have been told, this is where Kathleen was baptised as a baby. But what I want to ask is not why we are in this church but why anyone would want to get married in any church at all. Not to put too fine a point on it – why we are in a Christian place of worship – or as Richard Dawkins might ask, 'What does God have to do with it?'

Complication: After all – much as we love them – Kathleen and David are both just rather unusual bubbles of protoplasm in the evolutionary soup, and having climbed out of the primal slime, they have been attracted by each other's pheromones. As you all doubtless know, pheromones are naturally occurring substances the fertile body excretes externally, conveying an airborne message to trigger a response from the opposite sex of the same species. Pheromones were first defined in 1959 as chemical substances excreted by animals to trigger reproductive behavioural response from a recipient of the same species.

In fact, having been friends as children they met again some three years ago at a New Year's Eve party and the first thing a biologically-determined Kathleen said to David was 'I do like your pheromones!'

Sudden shift: To which David replied, 'Come then, my love, my lovely one, come. My dove, hiding in the clefts of the rock, in the coverts of the cliff – show me your face, let me hear your voice; for your voice is sweet and your face is beautiful.'

Good news: The beautiful words of the Song of Songs point us beyond the chemical nuts and bolts of being two human beings predetermined by biological urges and take us into our experience of the sublime: 'For love is strong as Death, jealousy relentless as Sheol. The flash of it is a flash of fire, a flame of the Lord himself. Love no flood can quench, no torrents drown.'

Romantic love can be all about pleasing oneself – loving another only for the physical or emotional pleasure that the relationship offers, but genuine unselfish human love takes human beings beyond themselves into a world for which there is no language to do it justice. Philosophers talk about the experience of transcendence and theologians talk about the experience of God. For God is love. And love is God. Love is not just one of God's many attributes. It is God himself. When we say that God is all-powerful, we mean that love is all-powerful. When we say that God is present everywhere we mean that his love fills everything. When we say that God is eternal, we mean what St Paul meant in the passage we heard from 1 Corinthians when he wrote that 'Love does not come to an end.' And if Kathleen and David, or any of us, want our relationships to weather the storms that inevitably threaten love from time to time, then we can do no better than to ponder the description of love in that same passage. 'Love is always patient and kind; it is never jealous; love is never boastful or conceited; it is never rude or selfish; it does not take offence, and is not resentful. Love takes no pleasure in other people's sins but delights in the truth; it is always ready to excuse, to trust, to hope, and to endure whatever comes.'

Unfolding: Kathleen and David are making a lifelong commitment to each other. At the heart of the Christian faith, there is a love that does not end. We can see this love in the love of the man who, more than any other human-being, 'delighted in the truth'. He was ready to excuse even his murderers because they did not understand what they were doing. He trusted the Father's love to the end, never giving up hope and ready to endure everything for those he loved.

Kathleen and David, if you want the joy of today to last a lifetime, then strive to remain in the kind of love Jesus was speaking about in the Gospel I have just read: 'Remain in my love. If you keep my commandments, you will remain in my love... This is my commandment: love one another, as I loved you.

***

Preparation Process for Lucy and Andrew's Wedding

The Gospel reading for the wedding of Lucy and Andrew was John 2:1-11. The story of the Wedding Feast of Cana was chosen because it was seen as a beautiful story that associated Jesus and his mother with a wedding celebration, bringing a blessing on the couple who were to be married. This was a text on which I had preached a number of times before, so the information in the commentaries was of secondary importance to my wish to lead the congregation, using a narrative preaching methodology, from a consideration of their expectations of this particular wedding through to a consideration of the comparative circumstances of the Wedding at Cana of Galilee in the first century. In particular, the honour/shame dimension of running out of wine provided important elements to the homiletic plot. Other key points included the fact that the miracle was primarily an initiative of Jesus himself. Moreover the outline of the literary form of the Gospel text, as first as set out by Rudolf Bultmann, begins with the problem of there being no wine. I also wished to stress the link between the miracle and the saving event of Christ's death and resurrection.

My homiletic plan was structured in 'moves', along lines suggested by David Buttrick in his *Homiletic:*

Moves and Structures. The first move began with a life-centred introduction, comparing the wedding of Lucy with the wedding in the Gospel and exploring the same problematic issues as for the wedding of Kathleen and David: why people today should marry and why they should wish to commit themselves with the vows integral to Christian marriage. The Good News paralleling the miracle at Cana focuses on the power of Jesus Christ to change our lives. The development and application of this pointed to the love of God shown in Christ as providing the example and inspiration for the marriage liturgy of Lucy and Andrew, enabling them to emulate the foolishness of God's love in their relations to each other. References to the other two readings underline the character of this love.

Text of the Homily for Lucy and Andrew's Wedding

Move one: A life-centred narrative and a problem requiring resolution

Today we have a tale of two weddings – two wedding stories to compare. One of them is a very famous one that happened in a place called Cana in Galilee nearly two thousand years ago, and another taking place in this church today – that may end up being nearly as famous! Questions need to be asked about both weddings.

First, it is by no means clear why people should get married or why, if they do, they should invite Jesus to be one of the guests. Now it is not difficult to understand why the couple in the Gospel story got married. Nearly everybody got married in those days and the two families probably arranged the marriage. Today it is not so simple. Many choose not to get married. In our less community-conscious age, love between two people can be life-long or not, officially registered or not. Some have the opinion that it concerns only the two persons involved. Marriage is one life-style choice among others. Given many unhappy marriages and the growing divorce rate, it is easy to understand that many decide not to marry. Only people like Andrew and Lucy, who are very sure of each or, are brave enough to take the plunge! But having decided to get married, why invite Jesus to be one of guests?

The Gospel doesn't tell us why Jesus and his mother were there. Maybe they were relatives or friends of the couple. Everybody here is a relative, or a friend of Andrew or Lucy or both. But why have Andrew and Lucy decided to invite Jesus? Why have they decided to have a Christian ceremony? If you listen to them when they make their vows you may well wonder. Note what that they will be committing themselves to – a life-long, sexually exclusive relationship when they know quite well that, with the best will in world, many good people – as well as some bad ones – seem to find this ideal impossible to keep. And note what they will not be saying. They will not be saying, 'I will be true to you if you treat me right, if you are never unfaithful or unkind, if you are always as nice and as beautiful as you are now.' No. Christian marriage involves making an unqualified commitment. Boats will be burned. No way back!

So why have Andrew and Lucy decided to invite Jesus to their wedding? Well, ask Andrew and Lucy. Maybe it was to please their parents. Maybe it was for the photo opportunity. Maybe it was a way of making their wedding more solemn, more memorable. Not one of those ideas is altogether bad but here are my ideas on why it was a good idea to invite Jesus to their wedding.

Move two: He can turn water into wine!

So, here we go! He can turn water into wine! That couldn't have been the reason that Jesus was invited to the wedding at Cana because they did not know that they were going to run out of wine or that Jesus would be able to help them. I have been told that any one who has been around Andrew and Lucy during the last few months must know that it is very unlikely that anything has been forgotten. Preparation has been meticulous, bordering on the obsessive. And there is no doubt that the wine has not been forgotten. There is no need for Jesus to provide the wine this time! Or maybe there is. The Gospel story is richly symbolic. Jesus changes our reality. In Jesus, God became one of us so as to change the water of our lives into wine. St Paul says that he 'became poor to make us rich'. He became poor by being born in Bethlehem. He became poor when he died for us on the cross and he made us rich when he rose again in power on Easter day. He really made it possible to change our water into wine – but how?

Move three: Application

Jesus loves us so unreservedly that he provides the example and the means to love and care for each other beyond what is possible in the natural order of things. That is the best reason for Andrew and Lucy to have invited Jesus to come to their wedding – and not just to their wedding but to come into every day of their lives together. If they pray together, if they ask Jesus to be their brother and their friend he will perform miracles for them. The water at Cana represents what is possible in the natural order of things. Wine is the love spoken about in the Song of Solomon – love that

87

'is strong as death', love that 'many waters cannot quench' and the floods 'cannot drown'. Wine is the love that we heard about in the second reading – love that 'is patient... kind... not envious or boastful or arrogant or rude...' Love that 'bears all things, believes all things, hopes all things, endures all things'...love that 'never ends'. That is the love that we pray for Andrew and Lucy.

***

Feedback on the Two Weddings

After the wedding of Kathleen and David the feed-back on the homily, which was informal proved to be generally positive. The guests found the homily entertaining and challenging. In an attempt to research reactions to the wedding homily in greater detail, the feedback for the homily at Lucy and Andrew's wedding was solicited from a group selected for the purpose, meeting some time after the wedding with memories refreshed by a video recording of the wedding. The group included the bride and groom, Teresa, a brides-maid, who attends Mass reasonably regularly and has firm Christian convictions; the best man, Rick who is an agnostic, Sam who is a practising Anglican and Jon who is an articulate atheist. Sam and Jon live together and have a child. It seems clear that Sam would much rather that she and Jon were married and the difference of opinion between them was evident in the discussion. Teresa and Jon, like Lucy, are graduates in professional employment. Andrew manages an on-line retail business and Rick is a plumber. Questions were as follows:

1. Was there anything in the homily that particularly struck you or moved you or that you thought interesting or useful?
2. Was there anything in the homily that might have altered or confirmed your attitude towards Christianity or the Church?
3. Was there anything in the homily that might have altered or confirmed your attitude towards the institution of marriage?
4. Was there anything in the content or the delivery of the homily that made you feel alienated or annoyed?
5. In what ways might the homily have been better preached?

In answer to the first question, the group gave a generous appraisal of the relaxed and entertaining style of the preacher and most of the group regarded the approach as successfully involving everyone. Jon, however thought that reference to sexual fidelity was 'a bit iffy' and inappropriate for a wedding sermon and resisted the impression that marriage was in any way superior to cohabitation. Members of the group discussed the effect of the preaching on their attitude towards Christianity or the Church. The question was not answered directly but the two avowed unbelievers claimed at least not to have been put off Christianity by it. Sam suggested that the approach was inclusive and the group seemed to assent to this.

On the effect of the homily on attitudes towards the institution of marriage, existing attitudes seem to have been confirmed. Sam considered that the homily rightly stressed the seriousness of Christian marriage and Teresa saw the link between the unconditional love of God and the unreserved commitment suggested by the Christian ideal of marriage.

There were interesting answers to the question as to whether there was anything in the content or the delivery of the homily that made them feel alienated or annoyed. Rick misunderstood the scriptural and theological significance of Christ 'becoming poor so as to make us rich', and seemed to have perceived it as an implied criticism of his own economic aspirations. Jon returned to defensive mode and objected again to what he saw as the implied, although not stated, disparagement of non-marital domestic arrangements. The Christian teaching on the indissolubility of marriage was also questioned.

Criticism of the homily was generous but the bride-groom wondered whether the preaching did not go on for too long for those not accustomed to Church services. Rick concurred with this and added that he struggled with some of the unfamiliar words and concepts.

I was gratified that the feedback for both weddings was so positive. The formal feedback for the second group had the advantage of taking place after an inter-val of time so that the judgements were less affected by the general euphoria immediately consequent upon the marriage celebration. As with all homilies however, whether preached to regular worshippers or to those on the margins of Christian faith, the effect of the preaching is not strictly measurable. Whilst the preacher must make every effort to reach out to the imagination of his hearers, the ultimate harvest of the seed that is sown remains known only to God.

CHAPTER 7

'Lazarus is Dead':
Preaching at Funerals

One of the two homilies given here was prepared for a funeral service celebrated outside of Mass and the other for a Memorial Mass. In both cases the deceased as well as most of the family and friends attending the services had, at most, only tenuous links with Catholic faith or practice. Faced with such a situation, the preacher becomes aware that no common reference points or background knowledge can be assumed and the preacher may find it hard to find any 'common cause' beyond the human focus of sadness and confusion in the face of loss.

Even when the funeral is for a practising Catholic, the preacher may sometimes find it difficult to communicate a confident affirmation of Easter hope. Bereavement can have a devastating effect even in a community of faith and the preacher is not immune from this. The circumstances of funeral services for the lapsed and the semi-lapsed are often even more challenging. The film 'Four Weddings and a Funeral' may have had four weddings to one funeral, but in an increasingly secular society there are probably four funerals for every church wedding or christening! The reality is that we live in a largely post-Christian society in which, although many seem to be able to affirm their sexual relationships or celebrate the birth of a child without recourse to religious rites, when it comes to death they can respond to the pain of losing a loved one only with the half-remembered language and symbolism of a Christian funeral.

In the Church of England the vast majority of funerals are for non-churchgoers and the figures in the Catholic Church in this country probably run a close second. If the statistics on mass attendance in England and Wales are at all accurate in showing a decline from 2,114,219 in 1966 to just over 800,000 in 2006, it is to be expected that a large number of 'Catholic' funerals will be for Catholics who have not had any contact with the Church for some years.

In such circumstances the preacher has the task of meeting the challenge and the opportunities of the occasion. *The Order of Christian Funerals* spells out the goal powerfully and clearly enough: 'In the face of death, the Church confidently proclaims that God has created each person for eternal life and that Jesus, the Son of God, by his death and resurrection, has broken the chains of sin and death that bound humanity. Christians celebrate the funeral rites to offer worship, praise, and thanksgiving to God for the gift of a life which has now been returned to God, the author of life and the hope of the just.' This may be an accurate and an inspirational description of what happens at the memorial Mass for a committed Catholic where the majority of the mourners are Catholic families and friends, often members of the same parish congregation. Faced with a congregation unfamiliar with the liturgy or symbolism of the Eucharist, or with a confused group of mourners at the crematorium with a congregation in which nobody seems to be familiar even with the Lord's Prayer – the preacher may feel that the challenge dwarfs the opportunities!

One or more pastoral visit, spending time meeting with the bereaved can provide the preacher with the opportunity to find out as much as possible, not only about the deceased, but also about those who will be present at the funeral service.

The Order of Christian Funerals specifies that 'the Church calls each member of Christ's Body – priest, deacon, layperson – to participate in the ministry of consolation'. The homily should represent a continuance of this 'ministry of consolation'. As at any homily, the preacher will see an opportunity to witness to a faith that is understood as a way of interpreting the world 'not as a hostile and evil place but as the creation of a loving God, who did not allow it to destroy itself but sent his Son to rescue it' and – as for any homily – the preacher preparing a funeral homily will need, before interpreting the chosen Scripture texts, to address the equally important issue of interpreting the congregation because 'only when preachers know what a congregation needs to hear will they be able to communicate what a congregation needs to hear' (*Fulfilled in your Hearing:* 7).

Such an approach should exclude generic, off the peg homilies on any occasion – not least at funerals. However the introduction to *The Order of Christian Funerals* specifies that 'There is never to be a eulogy'. Instead, 'Attentive to the grief of those present, the homilist should dwell on God's compassionate love and on the paschal mystery of the Lord, as proclaimed in the Scripture readings. The homilist should also help the members of the assembly to understand that the mystery of God's love and the mystery of Jesus' victorious death and resurrection were present in the life and death of the deceased and that these mysteries are active in their own lives as well. Through the homily, members of the family and community should receive consolation and strength to face the death of one of their members with a hope nourished by the saving word of God'.

American Catholic homileticist, Fr Thomas J. Scirghi SJ, rightly insists that 'the meaning of a sacramental celebration is distorted when we shift the focus from God to the individual...' and 'nowhere is this confusion more glaring than when the funeral homily is replaced by a eulogy... The preacher needs to consider what it is that he is calling the people of God to celebrate today: either the promise of eternal life with Jesus Christ, or the past life of the deceased.' He goes on to ask 'Is the focus of the homily on the Lord or is it on the deceased? Some funeral homilies provide a lengthy and detailed account of the person's accomplishments and attributes, along with some peccadilloes thrown in for good humour. In this case the homily tends to sound more like a secular testimonial speech for a good citizen rather than a message of faith.' (http://www.catholic,net/rec/Periodicals/Feb 2000/funeral.html)

The reason for resorting to eulogy rather than homily can easily be the well-grounded fear of the opposite extreme that, in Father Scirghi's words 'the homily will sound too formal, too general, or not personal enough' – a danger that Father Scirghi seems to underestimate. Clearly the homily should be primarily a 'message of faith' rather than a eulogy, but the way the message is couched will be determined by what the preacher has learnt about the faith and the life of the deceased and his or her relationship with those who will be present at the funeral. 'The homilist should also help the members of the assembly to understand that the mystery of God's love and the mystery of Jesus' victorious death and resurrection were present in the life of the deceased…' Clearly this needs to involve some direct reference to the details specific to the person who has died. For example, there is little point in emphasising the reward of steadfast Christian faith in the case of a deceased person whose faith was apparently almost as non-existent as that of the majority of the congregation. In such a case the stress might be better placed on the grace and the mercy of God already evident in the life of the one who is mourned. This would not make the homily a eulogy but rather a witness to the Christian hope that corresponds to what a specific congregation 'needs to hear'. In many cases the family will request an opportunity for a eulogy proper which can be best provided for before or after the service, along with any favourite secular music or readings – as far the timetable of the church or crematorium allows.

Exegesis of Those Attending the Funeral Services:

The two examples of a funeral homily given here are based on actual funerals with the names and the pastoral details changed. One of them was prepared for a funeral service celebrated outside of Mass and the other for a Memorial Mass. In both cases the deceased as well as most of the family and friends attending the services had, at most, only tenuous links with Catholic faith or practice. Faced with such a situation, the preacher becomes aware that no common reference points or background knowledge can be assumed and may find it hard to find any 'common cause' beyond the human focus of sadness and confusion in the face of loss.

Remembering Maria:

Maria had apparently last attended Mass in her native Hungary, before leaving for England, in 1948. She had been married in a registry office to a non-practising Jew and together they had brought up three daughters, none of whom professed any religious belief. Residual Catholic sentiment was expressed by the rosary that Maria cherished and by her sometimes going to Catholic churches while on holiday to light a candle. The congregation at the crematorium represented three generations of the family and the Buddhist Thai carer of the Jewish husband.

During conversations with the family it was learnt that Maria loved travel stories and travel programmes. Her family had fond memories of her as a person with an infectious sense of fun. In particular they had relished the happiness they had shared with her on family holidays and at Christmas celebrations.

Remembering Jo:

Jo was an elderly Irish man who had largely left his Catholic practice behind when he left Ireland some fifty years ago. Jo was a heavy smoker and eventually died of emphysema in a local hospital where he requested and received the last rites of the Church. His wife had died some years before, his son and daughter were both university lecturers with a thoroughly secular outlook on life. The two grandchildren were teenagers with no religious background beyond RE lessons and school assemblies in the state school system. An elderly sister and a brother who had flown over from Ireland for the service were both practising Catholics.

In his youth Jo had been an active and a sociable man but an accident had rendered him permanently disabled and his children remembered him chiefly for his love of crosswords and his addiction to watching football and horseracing on the television. Although occasionally irascible, Jo had borne his disability stoically and even in his final illness he had focussed his attention primarily not on his own suffering but on the people that he loved and the things that interested him.

The Readings and Interpretive Technique for the Homily for Maria:

The readings for Maria's crematorium service were 1 John 3:1-3 ('Think what love the Father has lavished on us') and John 14:1-6 ('Do not let your hearts be troubled').

A reading of commentaries on the 1 John 3:1-3, emphasised that 'the Father makes us his children now' affirming the gratuitousness of the Father's love in calling us his children and that the writer 'does not tell us what we shall be; he is interested in the present fact and future glory to be believed'. Meanwhile a commentary on John 14 laid stress on the sense of foreboding on the eve of Christ's death, the understandable consternation of the disciples after the events, commands and prophecies of chapter 13 which 'must be overcome by a renewal of faith'.

The method of preaching adopted appears to be an example of 'line by line preaching' taking the listeners through the key verses of the two readings. In fact this traditional format conceals an inductive and dialogal form, beginning with reminiscences about Maria and suggesting ways in which God was present in her life. Uncertainty in the face of death is met by the admission of uncertainty about the nature of life beyond death in 1 John 3:3 and the assertion that 'we shall be like him'. As the homily moves to verses from John 14, it considers the reassurance offered by Jesus in the face of death (his own and Maria's) and identifies with the uncertainty of Thomas in finding this reassurance less than totally convincing. The contrasting last move of the homily offers the vision of Jesus who is no outsider to our pain and who is the way to the Father offering us a Truth and a Life that is bigger than death.

***

Text of the Homily for Maria

We have heard that Maria loved travel stories and travel programmes – and now she has gone on a journey herself – a journey that we will all join her on sooner or later. The journey, from start to finish was always a journey to God – a journey to a loving Father.

'Think of the love that the Father has lavished on us, by letting us be called God's children; and that is what we are.'

I would like to invite all those who knew Maria to reflect on the happiness and laughter that she gave them. I would like to suggest to you that each such moment was a sacrament of the Father's love; a sign of his love in her life.

Think of the love that the Father has lavished on us.

Children enjoy the games and the laughter that they share and part of the joy of being God's children is the happiness we get from each other. Christians believe that this human joy can give us a small inkling of the joy to come.

'My dear people, we are already the children of God but what we are to be in the future has not yet been

revealed; all we know is, that when it is revealed we shall be like him because we shall see him as he really is.'

We cannot imagine what it is like for Maria now or what it will be like for us when we join her – when our travel story is complete. And we cannot imagine what happiness we will have when we see God as he really is – the unimaginable joy and fulfilment of being at one with the boundless ocean of God's love.

In the Gospel I have just read, Jesus was approaching his own death on the cross. He told his disciples: *'Do not let your hearts be troubled. Trust in God still, and trust in me. There are many rooms in my Father's house; if there were not, I should have told you.'*

But our hearts are troubled. The Christian hope sounds grand but can I really believe it? Is it not just wishful thinking? And even if it is true, that doesn't alter the fact that Maria has gone away, leaving only memories, fear of our own deaths and the emptiness that afflicts anyone who loses someone they love.

But Christians believe that Jesus is not an outsider to our pain and our doubt – he experienced it himself and blazed a trail for us all the way to his resurrection and glory.

Jesus was with Maria on every step of her way – in all her prayers when she went into churches alone to light her candles, in her work, joys and the sufferings: from her baptism in Hungary when she became a child of God, in the hardships and drudgery of her early life and in all the work she did for others; in her joys that she gave and received from her husband David and her children and grandchildren and all the members of her extended family, often more like a mother than an auntie; and finally in her sufferings too, Jesus had been there before her – Jesus, the Way, the Truth and the Life – Jesus who is the way to the Father – a Father who loves Maria even more than any of us can. Jesus shows us the truth about God and about ourselves and through Jesus God offers something bigger than death. It is through Jesus that we can hope that Maria now comes to the Father who has lavished so much love upon us all. May she rest in peace.

The Readings and Interpretive Technique for the Funeral Homily for Jo

At the memorial Mass for Jo, the readings were Wisdom 3:1-9 ('The Souls of Righteous'), 1 John 3:1-3 and John 11:17-21 (the raising of Lazarus). The homily was structured using the approach proposed by Eugene Lowry with his five part methodology of conflict, complication, sudden shift, good news, and unfolding, giving examples and analogies.

The primary text for the homily was to be the dialogue between Jesus and Martha just prior to the raising of Lazarus. Maloney's commentary (*The Gospel According to John,* 322-324) unravels the conflicting mixture of faith, hope and misunderstanding which underlie Martha's side of the conversation and this seemed to provide an inductive approach suggesting some parallel to the conflict of emotions felt by Jo's family and friends. The implied criticism of Jesus in Martha's words 'If you had been here my brother would not have died' seem to capture the complication of the sense of Christ's absence often experienced with the loss of a loved one. Moreover the hope of being with Jo in heaven seems remote and deferred, corresponding to Martha's unenthusiastic 'I know that he will rise again at the resurrection of the just on the last day'. Moreover his sufferings remain inexplicable and unfair. A commentary on Wisdom 3:1-9 emphasises that the sufferings of the just are testing rather than punishment and that although 'the just seem to have died... they are really alive with God.'

However the sudden shift from uncertainly and incomprehension comes with the assertion by Jesus that he is 'the resurrection and the life'. This shift leads to the good news developed by a reference back to the parallel reassurance that we are the children of a loving Father in 1 John 3:1-3. The homily closes with an application to the liturgical context of the homily and to the real presence of Christ in our lives, in the Eucharist and to Jo.

***

Text of the Funeral Homily for Jo

Conflict: Everyone here has come to this service with memories of Jo. But remembering Jo will not bring him back to us except to our imagination. It may seem odd that at this service we are remembering Jo by remembering Jesus. The Catholic Mass is a way in which we remember Jesus and Catholics believe that remembering Jesus in this way does indeed make him present – and not only to the imagination. This is because he is the resurrection and the life.

Complication: When he was on his way to raise Lazarus from the grave Jesus met Martha and Mary – sad, as we are today, about the loss of someone they loved very much. 'If you had been here my brother would not have died.' Death seems so cruel that it makes us wonder why Jesus seems to be absent from our world. But maybe there is something else: 'Your brother,' said Jesus, 'will rise again'.

For Martha, like us, that doesn't seem quite good enough 'I know that he will rise again on the last day!'

We experience pain: the pain of losing a loved one, even after 86 years: years that included sadness as well as happiness, the loss of his wife after her 10 years of diabetes and final illness, his accident and loss of the use of his legs and the final weeks of his illness with all that that involved. The sadness we feel at the loss of a father, a grandfather or a friend seems too great for such a long term solution like rising 'on the last day'. The souls of the righteous may be in the hands of God but for us, like the unwise, they seem to die.

'The great by and by' is just not good enough to take away the hurt.

Sudden shift: Then Jesus puts Martha right – puts us right: 'I am the resurrection and the life.'

But because we cannot imagine what the resurrection of Jesus will mean for us, the words of St John in the second reading speak to us 'We are already the children of God. What we are to be in the future has not been revealed. All we know is that when he is revealed, we shall be like him because we shall see God as he really is.'

Good News: Just notice that all that uncertainty, all the not knowing about death, is alright – because we are God's children. We are God's children because Jesus, the resurrection and the life, is really our brother. If we can believe that God loves us as his children then we are already the children of God.

Unfolding: And this is our 'Good News' that Jesus is alive now – the power of his death and rising is not something that religious people expect at the end. It is a present reality for anyone of us when we lay hold on it with trust and love. Christianity teaches that, in Jesus, God comes right to centre of our lives sharing in our pain, sharing in our dying – Jesus is the one who was dead and who is alive. He is present with us all the time and it is that presence that we celebrate in the Mass in which Catholics believe that he is becomes present to us in a special way under the outward forms of bread and wine.

(PAUSE) As we remember Jo, we reflect that Christ is present to him now and we place him in the loving care of the God who raised Jesus from the dead.

SECTION III
Preaching Across the Divide

CHAPTER 8

Preaching Across the Ecumenical Divide: 'The Strange Exorcist'

'Teacher,' said John, 'we saw a man driving out demons in your name and we told him to stop, because he was not one of us.' 'Do not stop him,' Jesus said. 'No one who does a miracle in my name can in the next moment say anything bad about me, for whoever is not against us is for us.'

(Mark 9:38, New International Version)

'Ecclesial communities which have not preserved the valid Episcopate and the genuine and integral substance of the Eucharistic mystery, are not Churches in the proper sense; however, those who are baptised in these communities are, by Baptism, incorporated in Christ and thus are in a certain communion, albeit imperfect, with the Church.'

(Dominus Jesus, 38-39)

The reflections offered here developed out of an invitation to preach at an ecumenical event in rural England. The sermon was to be preached at St James' Church, Stedham, in Sussex, at an ecumenical service organised for 'Rother Valley Churches Together'. The invitation was, in the first instance, given to the UK based 'College of Preachers', an ecumenical organisation existing to promote good preaching in the United Kingdom. The College was requested to find a preacher who would address the issue of how Christian churches regarded each others' ministries. This presented a particular challenge to me as a Roman Catholic ordained minister in the light – or the shadow! – of the recent Congregation for the Doctrine of the Faith (CDF) document, which reiterates terminology in the earlier CDF document *Dominus Jesus* of 2000 which had already been perceived as insensitive by many. How could I try both to preach an inclusive and affirming ecumenical message and, at the same time, accurately reflect the current mind of the Roman Catholic Church? The scripture readings that I chose for the service consisted of Numbers 11:25–29 in which Moses deals with the issue of unauthorised prophets, and Mark 9:38–43, in which the disciple, John, protests to Jesus about someone who was not part of the in-group of disciples, casting out devils in his name.

I will attempt first to examine the relevance of these two biblical texts for modern Christian ecumenism. In the Marcan pericope of 'the strange exorcist' I perceived a threefold pattern in which sentiments of exclusion are challenged by prophetic inclusion which is then, in turn, moderated and diluted by subsequent interpretation. This threefold pattern is seen again in the official documents of the Roman Church. In the first instance the value of Anglican and reformed ordained ministry was denied over more than five centuries. A new approach was then prophetically affirmed in the Vatican II documents, particularly in the Decree on Ecumenism, *Unitatis Redintegratio.* Then, with the passage of years since the Council, it becomes possible to discern a retreat to a less affirmative attitude in the most recent Roman documents.

The approach adopted in preparing a sermon sought to engage with, and speak in the name of three

Christian traditions: Anglican; Roman Catholic and Free Church. In the text of the sermon each tradition is seen as struggling to transcend a sense of identity which affirms elements that might seem to exclude the other two traditions, or to disparage their ordained ministries. I will suggest that the common baptismal ministry of the baptised Christian is primary and that the common focus for unity consists in engaging in the struggle for peace and justice, casting out demons in the name of Jesus Christ.

The Biblical Texts

The lectionary compilers and the biblical scholars concur in linking Mark 9:38-43 with Numbers 11:25-29.[55] In both cases the message is one in which a great teacher rebukes factional and exclusivist sentiments in favour of an attitude of tolerance and inclusion. As one commentator remarks, 'it is ironic that this advice appears shortly after the account of the disciples' failure to cast out a demon in 9:14-29.'[56] More immediately before this account in 9:34-36, Jesus has rebuked the disciples, comparing their spiritual hubris with the humility of a child. This sequence provides not only the verbal link ('in your name') but also 'another example of the disciples' failure through arrogance to understand the nature of their mission of service'.[57] The context of the subsequent warning against causing the 'little ones' to stumble in verse 42 can be taken to refer to the disciples, to children or indeed to those like the alien exorcist. Each of these three can be identified with 'the little ones who believe in me'.

Failure of the Disciples	Verbal link: 'in your name'	'Little Ones who believe in me'
Argument over who would be first (9:33-37)	Child to be received 'in my name' (9:37)	Children as the little ones (9:37)
Complaint over 'strange exorcist' (9:38)	Demons cast out in Christ's name' (9:39)	Believers outside the circle of the disciples as the little ones (9:40)
		The disciples as the little ones (9:41)

In later Christian centuries commentators squirmed and wriggled to avoid the obvious inclusivism of Christ's words. For example, Augustine expressed concern that the saying 'Anyone who is not against us is for us' should not be taken to be 'contrary to that where he says, 'he who is not with me is against me' and adds that the disciples, 'ought to have forbidden his being without their society and thus persuaded him of the unity of the Church, but they should not have forbidden that in which he was one with them, that is his commendation of the name of their Lord and Master by the expulsion of devils'.[58] Likewise, the tenth century Byzantine patriarch Theophylactus remarks that 'some unbelievers seeing that the name of Jesus was full of virtue, themselves used it and performed signs, though they were unworthy of Divine Grace; for the Lord wished to extend his name even by the unworthy'.[59]

Roman Texts

Centuries later Christians replicated the factional and exclusivist attitudes of the Apostle John when, in the fifteenth and sixteenth centuries, the churches of the Protestant Reformation developed new and various theologies of ordained ministry which placed the emphasis upon the ministry of the Word rather than on the celebration of the sacraments. In the polemic of the reformers those who celebrated the Mass were idolaters and blasphemers.[60] At the Council of Trent the Roman Catholic Church in turn regarded the clergy of the new churches not as 'true ministers of the Church but as thieves and robbers who have not entered through the door (John 10:1)'.[61]

In those of the new churches that retained an episcopal model the new bishops in these churches were in general not ordained by previously Roman Catholic bishops and even where they were, as in the case of Anglican and some Scandinavian Lutheran churches, no special value was placed upon the fact. The Anglican Prayer Book specified episcopal ordination of clergy but this was chiefly directed towards securing state control over the Church since the bishop was now an agent of the monarch as supreme governor of the Church of England.[62] It was only in the context of the challenge of more radically protestant movements in England that some of the Caroline divines asserted that episcopacy gave Anglicanism a special status over against other protestant churches. In the nineteenth century the founders of the Oxford movement taught that the apostolic succession, preserved in the Church of England, gave it a special Catholic character alongside the Roman Catholic and the Eastern Orthodox churches, with a priesthood ordained to celebrate the Eucharistic sacrifice.

This movement away from a protestant understanding of ministry was encouraged by some French and Belgian Catholics but received no encouragement at all from Rome and in 1896 Pope Leo XIII pronounced 'that ordinations carried out according to the Anglican rite have been, and are, absolutely null and utterly void'.[63] According to one ecumenical Catholic theologian this language of official refusal to recognise any positive elements in the churches of the Reformation left Catholic ecumenism 'in the quite lonely hands of a small band of theological pioneers'. Official attitudes and practices were structured by the conviction that non-Catholic Christians were the adversaries of our central religious and moral tenets. Canon 1399 symbolised this. It forbade the reading of books written by Protestants that expressly treated religious themes: 'the very separation of non-Catholics from the one true church constituted disparagement of their religious and moral thought'.[64]

The prophetic reversal of this attitude on the part of the Catholic Church came about with the Second Vatican Council's Decree on Ecumenism *Unitatis Redintegratio,* which asserted that 'very many of the significant elements and endowments which together go to build up and give life to the Church itself, can exist outside the visible boundaries of the Catholic Church: the written word of God; the life of grace; faith, hope and charity, with the other interior gifts of the Holy Spirit, and visible elements too...'.[65] While resisting a simple equation of sacramental worship and ministry in each and every church without distinction, the decree gives positive significance to liturgical actions in those churches, asserting that they 'most certainly can truly engender a life of grace in ways that vary according to the condition of each Church or Community. These liturgical actions must be regarded as capable of giving access to the community of salvation.' Speaking about the churches of the Reformation, the decree refers to 'many Communions, national or confessional,' which were 'separated from the Roman See' and notes that 'among those in which Catholic traditions and institutions in part continue to exist, the Anglican Communion occupies a special place'.[66] These separated churches of the West are characterised as ecclesial communities which 'we believe have not retained the proper reality of the Eucharistic mystery in its fullness, especially because of the absence of the sacrament of Orders. Nevertheless, when they commemorate His death and resurrection in the Lord's Supper, they profess that it signifies life in communion with Christ and look forward to His coming in glory. Therefore the teaching concerning the Lord's Supper, the other sacraments, worship and the ministry of the Church, must be the subject of the dialogue'.[67]

Such dialogue, developed over recent decades, has led to an amazing degree of convergence, particularly in relation to Lutheran-Roman Catholic and Anglican-Roman Catholic discussions. Although important issues of faith and order remained outstanding, in 1970 Pope Paul VI referred to the Anglican Church as 'a sister church', apparently putting it on the same level as the Eastern churches. However in his 1995

Encyclical '*Ut Unum Sint*' Pope John Paul II applied the term 'sister churches' only to the separated churches of the East.

The more recent Roman documents from the Congregation for the Doctrine of the Faith have been criticised for backtracking on the prophetic inclusiveness of Vatican II and Pope Paul VI. The 2007 CDF document ordered by Pope Benedict XVI reiterates the message of the earlier 2000 document *Dominus Jesus* by emphasising that the Eastern Churches were 'wounded' by not being in Communion with the See of Peter and that the churches of the Reformation could not be considered 'churches' in the proper sense of the word since they lacked 'valid' sacraments and the apostolic succession.

Neither document said anything much new as regards established Catholic understanding, but the tone and choice of vocabulary gave widespread offence. The defence that CDF documents were meant primarily for internal consumption among Catholic pastors and theologians ignored the fact that the documents would be open to negative interpretations by partners in the ecumenical dialogue. One such interpretation, from the Church of Ireland, expressed regret that discussion of Christian ecumenical relationships 'should be linked to issues of relationships between Christianity and other faiths' and claimed that this 'is to undermine the real measure of communion that already exists between those who have been baptised as Christians'.[68] The statement that 'Ecclesial communities that have not preserved the valid episcopate and the genuine and integral substance of the Eucharistic mystery are not churches in the proper sense' also drew a critical response from the former Archbishop of

Canterbury, Lord George Carey, who claimed that such sentiments failed to do justice to 'the deeper understanding that has been achieved through ecumenical dialogue and cooperation during the last thirty years', adding that the Anglican Church 'believes itself to be part of the one, holy, apostolic Church of Christ'. Lutheran Bishop Wolfgang Huber regarded the wording as a deliberate snub: after *Dominus Jesus* ecumenists on both sides made every effort to explain away the sentence after saying that it had been 'misunderstood' or was 'unfortunately worded', however 'this text repeats the same offensive wording. It is quite obviously deliberate'.[69]

Preparing the Sermon

To this background of disappointment and hurt over issues of 'validity' of orders and the status of denominations either as 'churches' or 'ecclesial communities' could be added the internal Anglican dispute over admission of women to the priesthood and episcopate, the subsequent refusal by some Anglicans to accept women's ordination and the numerically significant number of former Anglicans who have become Roman Catholics over this issue. Since the whole question of recognition of ministries appeared to be problematic I chose to introduce the sermon with a light hearted 'hook' based on the common experience of how people seek out community and a sense of belonging. Using the 'Lowry loop', I then constructed the sermon around headings of 'conflict', 'complication', 'sudden shift', 'good news' and 'unfolding' or application. The 'conflict' consisted of a sympathetic account of why different traditions are secure in their separated identities and the 'complication' in how this expressed itself in the partial failure to recognise the ordained ministries of other traditions – making the point that baptism remains the source of, and the authority for, the common ministry of all Christians. The 'sudden shift' came with the account in both scripture readings of the fact that prophecy and casting out of devils occurred outside received frameworks. The 'good news' was expressed in the respective responses, first of Moses and then of Jesus, to the exclusivist complaints of their followers. The final 'unfolding' drew upon the insight that the Christians were united in the name of Jesus and that they shared a common prophetic task of casting out modern 'devils' of violence, prejudice and injustice in his name.

The Text of the Sermon

Belonging

Belonging makes for security. If we find ourselves among strangers we start looking for some links with at least some of the individuals around us. Some of them may have a similar background or interests: they support the same team; went to the same school or college; share an enthusiasm for pot-holing, golf or watching the Simpsons.

Belonging makes for security. People who don't belong often lack that security.

Anglican Belonging

Belonging makes for security. Anglicans feel secure believing that they belong to a Church that has its roots deep in the culture and the soil of England. They trace their origins back to St Augustine of Canterbury who first brought the Gospel to England. They value the openness of Anglicanism that they believe helps them to combine all that is best in Catholicism with all that is valuable in the Reformation. Not only do they claim the saints of the undivided church but they can celebrate the memory of great souls like George Herbert and John Donne, William Temple and Trevor Huddleston, great theologians like John Jewell and Lancelot Andrewes or martyrs like Cranmer, Latimer and Ridley. Theirs is the Church of England and it is 'a goodly heritage'.

Roman Catholic Belonging

Belonging makes for security. Roman Catholics feel secure believing they belong to a Church that was founded by the Lord himself; teaching with his authority; making them one with holy men and women of every nation and culture over the last twenty centuries. They have had their share of scandals: inquisitions and crusades, corrupt popes and abusive priests, but if the Roman Catholic Church sometimes produces the worst it also manages to bring out the best too. The sacraments that nourish the faith of Roman Catholics has nourished not just spiritual giants like St Francis, St Teresa of Avila or St John of the Cross, fearless martyrs like Margaret Clitherow or Maximilian Kolbe, but so many wonderful ordinary men and women who lived the love of God to the full in the family of the Church – one Church, in one communion with the successors of Peter and the apostles.

Free Church Belonging

Belonging makes for security. Free Church Christians can pride themselves on being free from man-made traditions, on looking to God alone for help, to the Bible alone for guidance and to faith alone for salvation. They believe that they can clearly see the wood of the cross while others may have their view obscured by the trees. They know that their forebears brought to Christ many who were neglected by the established Church, and that their freedom in Church order contributed to the growth of democracy and human rights. Theirs is the family of Bunyan and Milton, of Whitfield and Wesley, of Spurgeon and Booth – of men and women who know Jesus Christ and him crucified and know that that message contains all that they really need to know.

Conflict

It is good to be on the inside, but that must mean that others are on the outside. I was asked to talk about how we recognise each other's ministries.

Complication

If we mean ordained ministries then, at first sight at least, quite simply, we don't recognise each others ministries. Free Church ministers who become Anglicans have to be re-ordained by a bishop. Among Anglicans there are differences over the ordination of women so that some Anglicans do not even recognise priests of their own church family. Anglican priests who become Roman Catholics have to be re-ordained if they are to become priests in the Roman Catholic Church. Of course this doesn't mean that we consider any other church's ministry worthless. Rather we are saying that they do have not the same currency everywhere. (I once got on a plane in Delhi with enough rupees to buy a slap up meal back in India but found that when I wanted to buy duty free on the plane I needed dollars, pounds or yen: 'We do not accept rupees here.')

Well at least most of us recognise each other's baptisms – and I believe that baptism is the basis for the ministry of every Christian. Although I once asked a 'White Russian' Orthodox priest whether he required re-baptism for Christians from other churches who might wish to join his and he replied, 'Always! We used to not baptise Roman Catholics but now they have guitar masses and we don't know what they believe!'

Sudden Shift: 'He was not one of us; we tried to stop him.'

So here we are each in our own small corner – you in yours and I in mine. But if our hearts and minds are open, we learn that God is working in all the corners! So what does an Anglican think when he or she hears that someone has been brought to Christ by the preaching of the Salvation Army? Or what does a Baptist say when he or she hears a Catholic bishop speaking out, saying things that he might have liked to hear his own minister say, or a Roman Catholic who hears of a miracle of healing taking place, not at Lourdes, but at an Pentecostal rally? Even in Old Testament times people were shocked to find that God could act beyond the ordered scheme of things. When the spirit came on seventy elders two men had stayed behind and the spirit came down on them though they had not gone to the Tent. So Joshua protested 'My Lord Moses, stop them!' And in the Gospel John says to Jesus, 'Master, we saw a man who is not one of us casting out devils in your name; and because he was not one of us we tried to stop him.'

Good News: 'Anyone who is not against us is for us.'

Moses answered Joshua 'Are you jealous on my account? If only the whole people of the Lord were prophets, and the Lord gave his Spirit to them all!' and Jesus answers John's complaint along similar lines. 'You must not stop him: no one who works a miracle in my name is likely to speak evil of me. Anyone who is not against us is for us.'

Application: One Father and One Task

So the vision we get from today's readings is of a sense of belonging that is inclusive – that rejoices when people we thought of as outsiders are seen to be doing God's work. People not signed up as prophets prophesy when the Spirit falls upon them and the name of Jesus has power even outside the circle of Peter and the Apostles. One of the signs of the Holy Spirit in our times is the movement for Christian Unity, based on the realisation that anyone who acknowledges Jesus as Lord is our sister or brother. It is the gifts of the Spirit and the name of Jesus that drives Christians back into unity with each other. If we are looking for what unites us it is the name in which we cast out devils – the name of Jesus Christ our brother who is our way to the Father who gives us the one Spirit who unites and heals. We share a common sonship and daughtership – St Augustine said of the Donatist Christians who had separated themselves from the mainstream Church of his day: 'They will cease to be our brothers and sisters only when they cease to say 'Our Father'.

But if we are united in who we are, we are also united by what we have to do. We have to cast out devils: the devils of unbelief and despair; of war and injustice; of prejudice and racism; of materialism and

119

hedonism and of everything that prevents God's children from being fully human. This is a ministry that all Christians have, a ministry to be exercised in the name of Christ who prayed that all his disciples might be one so that the world might see and believe.

CHAPTER 9

Preaching and the Israeli-Palestinian Conflict

For Zion's sake I will not keep silent, and for Jerusalem's sake I will not rest

(Isaiah 62:1)

Five gospels record the life of Jesus. Four you will find in books and one you will find in the Land they call Holy. Read the fifth gospel and the world of the four will open to you.

(Bargil Pixner OSB – Jerusalem 1992, attributed to St Geronimus.)

The Holy Land of Israel-Palestine introduces a range of problems, challenges and opportunities for preaching. These include the unfamiliar context and the historical, religious and cultural realities. Visiting the land of the Bible offers potential for more critically and historically based preaching. It also requires sensitivity both to the ecumenical and multi-faith background of the Holy Land as well as to the volatile and complex realities of Israeli-Palestinian conflict. Finally, it should involve awareness of the Living Stones, the local Palestinian Christians and their communities whose very survival is now threatened.[70]

The original setting of most of the Bible, including all of the Gospels and the first thirteen chapters of Acts, is the Holy Land. The term "Holy Land" refers primarily to modern Israel-Palestine but can also include those parts of Jordan, Syria and Egypt that form part of the Bible narrative. Visiting the Holy Land provides unique opportunities to the preacher because of the historical and geographical context from which the Gospel derives. The richness of background historical and archaeological material for biblical study is of great potential value to the preacher. However, such material alone cannot dictate the direction of the preaching. Approaches to preaching must take account of the "world in front of the text". This world includes the congregation with its cultural and religious background. It must also include the religious, social and political realities of the Holy Land itself, a land subject to rival claims by Israelis and Palestinians.

The religious life of observant Jews in Israel provides numerous reference points for the Christian preacher. Models of social and cultural life in the peasant society in which Jesus lived also find parallels in Palestinian and other Arab societies. Preachers who have visited the Holy Land or who have studied accounts of its geography and culture are able to draw on this in their preaching. For example, patterns of farming and of social life have until very recently remained largely unchanged over centuries. Watch-towers and landmarks survive to offer visual echoes of Old Testament symbols. Palestinian peasants farm olive groves and fig trees much as they did in the time of Jesus. Palestinian shepherds do not drive their sheep as western shepherds do – they lead them.

There are also a number of parallels between the society in which Jesus lived and peasant society in the Middle East today.[71] In common with most twenty-first century Palestinians, Jesus lived in an extended family, an economic unit in which parents controlled the choice of a marriage partner within a defined social group.[72] The bride lived with the bridegroom's family. Virginity in the bride before marriage[73] and faithfulness to her husband after it[74] were important elements in a code of shame and honour that operating at individual and family level. Promiscuity was abhorred, particularly in women,[75] and adultery was, in principle at least, punishable by death.[76] Inheritance rights for sons had relative priority over those of daughters.[77] These laws derived from the Pentateuch and are similar to those in Islamic Shari'ah law.[78] Another important element still surviving in Palestinian society is the patron-client relationship by which power, influence, inducement and commitment are exchanged between persons of unequal social standing.[79]

Ecumenical and Inter-Faith Approaches

The preacher who visits the Holy Land can identify a rich variety of, often competing, Christian communities present in, or coming to, the Holy Land today. Sensitivity to this requires a strong ecumenical awareness in preaching.[80] So, too, is an awareness of a wider pluralism of the three great religions – and by extension, of all religions. One of the primary religious realities of the Holy Land is that it is holy to the three faiths of Christianity, Islam and Judaism. Many Christian holy places are also revered by one or both of the other two faiths. Preachers may recognise the significance of some of these sites to Judaism and Islam. To do so requires not only constant reference to the often problematic history of relations between these faiths in past centuries but also to the conflict of the last sixty years.

For each of the three faiths Israel-Palestine has a

place that should encourage dialogue and mutual understanding. The reality is that over the centuries the holy city has witnessed massacres and continual rivalry for control by each of the three faiths at the expense of the other two. For Jews this is the land promised to Abraham and Moses, the land of David and Solomon. Long before modern Zionism succeeded in giving political significance to the Holy Land, Jerusalem served as a spiritual symbol of religious identity and of hope for Jews throughout the world. For Muslims Jerusalem, *Al Quds ash Sharif* is associated with the offering of Ishmael as a sacrifice by Abraham and also with the "furthest *qibla*", the destination of the prophet Muhammad on his miraculous night journey.

Opportunities abound for inter-faith preaching perspectives in sites associated with the Gospel stories. The traditional site of Christ's birth is a few hundred yards from the Jewish shrine of Rachel's tomb and the sound of the Muslim call to prayer provides a background sound to worship in the Church of the Nativity. The preaching of the Christmas Gospel can stress that Christians draw from the tradition of Judaism and that Muslims share with Christians a reverence for Christ and his Virgin Mother. The traditional site of the Last Supper was used as a mosque and in the same complex there is "the tomb of David" and, nearby, the "Chamber of the Holocaust", a memorial to the victims of the *Shoah*. This last includes a bar of soap made from human fat. The juxtaposition of this gruesome reminder of how the dignity of the human body can be degraded has been used as powerful homiletic counterpoint to the mystery of the sacramental Body of Christ celebrated a few yards away in the Franciscan Church of the Cenacle.

Historical and Political Issues

Preaching in the Holy Land itself takes place in an area of contested secular historical and political issues constantly confronting the pilgrim. Outside the Holy Land preachers will be concerned with matters of relevance to the local context for their preaching. Nevertheless, Israel-Palestine can never be far from the mind of any preacher or congregation, wheresoever situated. We live in a "global village" in which regional issues have planetary-wide significance. The Israeli-Palestinian conflict is just such an issue. In Christian preaching the biblical text itself constantly refers us back to the land that is proclaimed as in some special way the arena of God's revelation and saving actions in history. The fact that those who take sides in the modern Israeli-Palestinian conflict frequently invoke the Bible makes it even more difficult to ignore what is taking place in the land where it all began. Any preaching of the angel's Christmas message of peace could scarcely avoid reference to such events and still lay claim to be responsible or incarnational.

Preaching Resurrection and the Holy Land

The Resurrection of Jesus is the central element in the Christian message and the primary focus of the Christian pilgrimage to the Holy Land. Rival claims made for the site of Calvary and the Holy Sepulchre raise questions of a historical-critical nature. In addition the turf wars of the ancient churches in the precincts of the traditional site, the Church of the Holy Sepulchre and its rival, the Garden Tomb, pose challenges to ecumenism with issues of inter-faith and political theology never far away.

Christians value the Holy Land as the locus of the

death and the resurrection of Jesus – events that are central, not only to Christian pilgrimage, but to any preaching of the Gospel message. It is not possible to separate the cross from the resurrection and both the rival sites bring these two events together through the proximity of Golgotha and the tomb. However the Resurrection can be preached in a simplistic way as a happy ending that abolishes the cross, instead of making it at once a symbol of hope and of paradox. Such preaching is possible only if one ignores the enduring tragedies that must determine genuinely contextual preaching perspective.

Ever since the identification of the hill of Golgotha and of the tomb of Jesus in 348, the Church of Holy Sepulchre, built over the site of a temple of Aphrodite, has served as the central focus of pilgrimage for Catholic and Orthodox Christians. In 1883 General Gordon of Khartoum identified a rival site outside the Ottoman city walls off the Nablus Road. The claim for the Church of the Holy Sepulchre, disputed by some scholars, is more serious. Such ambiguity mirrors the historical evidence surrounding the Resurrection itself.

Moral ambiguities also appear. The downside of the fascinating liturgical pluralism that characterises the church of the Holy Sepulchre is to be seen in rivalry between Greek Orthodox, Latins and the four "Oriental Orthodox" communities who all manage to be fiercely competitive over inches of bricks and mortar. The consequence of these rivalries, deliberately encouraged by the Ottomans in the past and exploited more recently by the Israelis – produce not only sporadic rows and brawls but also cause neglect for the fabric of the Church itself on account of the difficulty of obtaining any consensus between the sects. Other ambiguities for pilgrims included the experience of droves of tourists shepherded by Israeli tour guides often displaying conspicuous lack of respect for beliefs that they do not share.

Many pilgrims have returned full of such negative experiences of the Church of the Holy Sepulchre. Worldwide, mention of the Holy Land today now conjures up images of tanks, roadblocks, missiles and suicide bombers. Perhaps it is a mistake to expect more from an empty grave. The Church of the Holy Sepulchre is called the *Martyrion*[81], a place that bears witness to the resurrection precisely by the absence of the Lord from the tomb. The earliest gospel testimony to the Resurrection ends with the holy terror of the women in the presence of the empty place where the Lord had been (Mk 16:8).

Unsurprisingly the contemplative atmosphere of the Garden Tomb conforms more readily to the sentimental expectations of many western pilgrims. There is no holy terror here and some Evangelical preaching is either innocent of political contextual awareness or imbued with a perspective that portrays occupation and oppression as fulfilment of God's promises for one people at the expense of another. By contrast the very awfulness of the *Martyrion* is in keeping with the tragedy all around. A few miles away at Yad Vashem the death of six million Jews is commemorated on land expropriated from Christian Palestinians in 1948. Two hours away, in Gaza, nine hundred thousand Palestinian refugees live under siege in squalor and acute deprivation amidst the wreckage of their homes in the most overcrowded place on earth. Not offering dignity or hope for the future, this dreadful place is a breeding ground for religious fanaticism and violence. Crucifixion did not end on Easter Day.

The key to preaching the Easter message in a Holy Land context is to hang on to the paradox that the place that witnesses to Christian hope is set in a land of ambiguity and calamity.[82] As such it is a sign of what it is like preaching beyond Jerusalem, Judaea and Samaria in the uttermost parts of the earth. From the *favelas* of Latin America to the killing grounds of Afghanistan come the cries of innocent victims. Easter faith is not blind but to be proclaimed faithfully, it must be preached in the context of the fear and ambiguity of the empty tomb.

This year in Jerusalem!

Preaching Applications:
'Bridges not Walls' and 'Take away the Stone'

Relating preaching to a current issue in Israel-Palestine, my first example of this approach is a homily for Year C, 21st Sunday after Pentecost (28th Sunday in Ordinary Time). In Luke 17:11-19 Jesus is 'passing along between Samaria and Galilee' (RSV). Following this route today, he might find he was walking along the line of the notorious wall being built on – and often well within – the Palestinian occupied territories, dividing Israelis from Palestinians, as well as separating some 7000 Palestinians from other Palestinians, according to which identity cards they possess.

The wall prevents farmers from getting to their land, doctors from their patients, workers from their homes, patients from their doctors, worshippers from places of worship and members of families from each other. In the words of Pope John Paul II, 'The Holy Land needs bridges and not walls.' Following the Lowry preaching methodology of looking for conflict and contradiction in the text we find that the conflict underlying the situation confronting Jesus in the Gospel passage is not far distant from the problems in the modern Holy Land. Relations between Samaritans and Jews were characterised by fear and hatred, rather as relations between Palestinians and Israelis are today. The fact of the ten lepers being 'lepers' presents an additional complication that strengthens the sense of the otherness of the grateful Samaritan leper. The sudden shift takes place in verse 17, 'Now he was a Samaritan.' The good news is in the response of Jesus to the man's gratitude in verse 19, 'Rise and go on your way, your faith has saved you.' The application is at once personal and political. The personal dimension derives from the fact that the preacher and everyone listening to the preacher are in the position of the ten 'lepers'. They are personally outsiders to God's grace until they encounter that grace in the words of Jesus and follow his instructions – even then they fail to express their gratitude. The ingratitude of the nine serves as the opportunity for Jesus to draw attention to the gratefulness of the Samaritan. The political application can be made to any or every one of the tragic situations in which Jesus needs to point out to us that his concern extends to those we fail to value and attempt to keep out. Within our society these can be identified as our social and economic inferiors, migrants, sufferers, or people with disability. On the international stage, the Samaritan leper is any one of the poorest living in the 'developing world', fenced out by unjust tariff agreements and with their predicament excluded from our attention by a media that focuses on the ephemeral and the self-serving.

All this offers so many legitimate avenues for the preacher's application of the inclusive message of the

Gospel. However the actual geographical locus of the event might also lead us to the existence of a wall where there should be a bridge. We prefer not to face up to our moral responsibility for the flip side of having established a state that guarantees 'the right of return' to people of one religion and culture, born anywhere in the world, but at the same time excludes millions of others who were born there or whose parents or grand-parents were born there. Meanwhile, those non-Jewish citizens of Israel who remain suffer systematic discrimi-nation in housing and employment, and those in the West Bank and Gaza are denied the rights specified as guaranteed for civilians living under military occupa-tion. The fact that there are Christians among these victims of Israeli government policies should make us even more concerned to engage in advocacy on behalf of the Palestinian people as a whole. In the modern context of the place where the miracle took place, the Samaritan represents to us the Palestinian people, excluded by walls and electric fences, denied the most basic human rights and largely invisible to the liberal conscience of the pulpit and the academy.

From this specific, anchored in the original theatre on earth of our redemption, we can generalise our message to speak a word of freedom to the victims of oppression throughout the world.

The congregation for both of these homilies was a College congregation which had already heard more about the sufferings of the Palestinians than might otherwise have been the case. In one or two cases this had aroused anxieties that the preacher was too parti-san in his approach but in general his concerns were shared by a largely liberal and educated congregation.

Text of Homily: Bridges, not Walls

Conflict and Complication

Travelling along the border between Samaria and Galilee today, Jesus would find he was walking along the line of the notorious wall being built on – and often well within – the Palestinian occupied territories, dividing Israelis from Palestinians, as well as Palestinians from Palestinians, according to which identity cards they possess.

Since 2 October 2003, the area between the wall and the 'Green Line', marking Israel's pre-1967 border, has been declared a 'closed military zone'. Approximately seven thousand residents in these closed areas are obliged to apply for permits to remain living in their homes. Since these permits are valid for six months only, it is now a privilege for Palestinians to live on their own land. The wall prevents farmers living outside the zone from getting to their land within it. Medical staff and international humanitarian organisations also have to apply for special permits. It also keeps workers from their homes, patients from their doctors, worshippers from their places of worship and members of families from each other. In the words of Pope John Paul II, 'The Holy Land needs bridges and not walls.'

Sudden Shift

Only one leper cured by Jesus came back to give thanks and he was a Samaritan. The fact he was a leper strengthens the sense of the otherness of the grateful Samaritan even more. The ingratitude of the nine serves as the opportunity for Jesus to draw attention to the gratefulness of the Samaritan: 'The other nine, where are they? It seems that no one has come back to give praise to God, except this foreigner.' This must have really shocked and surprised the Jewish people present quite as much as the healing of Naaman the Syrian would have surprised their ancestors.

Good News

And Jesus tells this outsider, this man who would have been regarded as a heretic and racial inferior, 'Stand up and go on your way, your faith has saved you.'

Application

The application for us is both personal and political. At the personal level you and I are the Samaritan leper. At our baptism Jesus told us 'Stand up and go on your way, your faith has saved you.' Until we hear the words of Jesus spoken to us personally we may feel we are outsiders to God's love.

At the political level there are so many situations where the concern of Jesus extends to those we fail to value and attempt to keep out – people for whom we should be building bridges instead of walls – social and economic inferiors, migrants, sufferers from AIDS or people with disability.

On the international stage, the Samaritan leper is any one of the poorest living in the 'developing world'. fenced out by unjust tariff agreements and excluded from our attention by a media that focuses on the trivial and the self-serving.

But as Paul tells us they cannot chain up God's news. And God's news is the good news that no one is an outsider to the healing Power of Christ. The message for us as we celebrate this Eucharist, and our message to the world, is the same message as that of Jesus to the

Samaritan leper, 'Stand up and go on your way, your faith has saved you.'

One further, brief illustration is offered. Further south, the wall comes to within a few yards of the tomb of Lazarus at *Al Azariah*, in biblical Bethany, the locus of John 11. This chapter provides the verses appointed for the Gospel passage on the Fifth Sunday in Lent in Year A in both the Roman and the Common Lectionary. Here the preacher can focus on the conflict and complication that draws tears from the bereaved Marthas and Marys of both the Palestinian and the Israeli communities. In response to the sterile grief of those who despair of a political settlement and who have no solution beyond the building of barriers, placing concrete slabs between peoples, we proclaim the words of Jesus, 'Take away the Stone.'[83] In the Holy Land, as elsewhere, this is the Gospel message of freedom in our troubled times: 'Take away the Stone'.

***

Text of Homily: Take away the stone!

Ezekiel 37:12-11, Romans 8:8-11, John 11:1-45

Conflict

When we think about an episode like the one I have just read, we may ask, 'What has it to do with me, or anyone I know?' Well, it has to do with me because I have been to where it happened. I have been there number of times. The last time I visited, Al Azariah (the Arabic name for Bethany) was in April. In my mind's eye I can see the steep hill running past the garden of the Franciscan Church where I have sat with pilgrim groups so many times listening to the reading of the story of the raising of Lazarus. Just past the garden you pass the Franciscan Church beside the ruins of much older churches and, between the Church and the Mosque, is a doorway with steep steps running down to the tomb.

Further up the hill still is the Greek Orthodox Church which is used only once a year on Lazarus Sunday. On that Sunday the Patriarch leads his congregation up the hill from the Orthodox Church half a mile away in the town. A procession of officials and religious leaders of every kind meet him. He goes to the entrance to the cave and he calls out in a loud voice, 'Lazarus, here! Come out!'

But I didn't need to have to have been to Bethany for it to have meaning for my life. The story is about me. Anyone who has ever lost someone that they loved will have wanted to complain to Jesus in just the same way that Mary and Martha did when Lazarus died, 'Lord, if you had been here, my brother would not have died.' And when those who follow Jesus lose a parent, a sister, a brother, son or daughter, husband, wife, friend or other loved one, outsiders may well echo the words of some of people there that day in Bethany, 'He opened the eyes of the blind man, could he not have prevented this man's death?'

Complication

'Your brother', said Jesus to Martha, 'will rise again.' If we believe in Jesus we have a future hope, but it is too far in the future? The pain is now. The final resurrection is a long way off and heaven is far away. Martha said, 'I know he will rise again at the resurrection on the last day.'

Sudden Shift

Jesus said:' I am the resurrection and the life. If anyone believes in me, even though he dies he will live, and whoever lives and believes in me will never die. Do you believe this?'

Good News

And Martha responds with faith, 'I believe that you are the Christ, the Son of God, the one who was to come into this world.'

And the pain of Martha and Mary is Jesus' pain too. Jesus wept; and the Jews said, 'See how much he loved him!' And he goes to the entrance to the cave and he tells them, 'Take away the stone.' He calls out to Lazarus and the dead man is alive!

Application

And this event is about me and it is about our world. It is about me because I am Lazarus. At baptism I was given a new life. And if I haven't taken hold of that gift then perhaps I need to answer the call to come out of the tomb. Jesus is standing at the entrance of the cave calling me to 'Come out!' And we don't need to wait until the resurrection on the last day to live this new life. If our baptism, our new life in Christ, is not a lived experience then we need to be converted – turned around, living out a new direction in our lives. And if it is a lived experience then we are indeed like a Lazarus, someone who is dead and come alive.

And this miracle is not just about me, about you, it is about our world and its problems. Still sighing, Jesus reached the tomb: it was a cave with a stone to close the opening. When I was last in Bethany a vast wall had been thrown up just a few yards from the tomb –

the infamous Israeli stone wall that keeps farmers from their fields, sick people from their doctors, clergy from their people, and members of a family from each other. Jesus said, 'Take the stone away.' Those of us who have come alive in Christ have a duty to strive for peace and justice to take away all the stones that prevent people from being fully human. To take away all the things that treat the living as though they were dead. Lazarus came out, his feet and hands bound with bands of stuff and a cloth round his face. Jesus said to them, 'Unbind him, and let him go free.'

In this Mass we celebrate Jesus who is the resurrection and the life. And he speaks to each one of us, calling out to our suffering hearts: 'Lazarus, Come out!' and he speaks out for all the people who are unjustly imprisoned and bound in our world – all the forces of oppression and injustice that afflict his sisters and brothers – and he tells any who will listen to 'Take the stone away.' 'Unbind them, to let them go free.'

Endnotes

1 Part of sermon 49, reproduced for the second reading for the Office of Readings for the memorial of St Bernadine of Siena, on 20 May.

2 Pope Benedict XVI, *Sacramentum Caritatis*, 2007, 139-40.

3 Ibid. St Bernadine of Siena, on 20 May.

4 *Presbyterorum Ordinis* 6.

5 Joseph Webb, *Preaching and the Challenge of Pluralism,* Chalice Press, St Louis, Missouri, 1998, 99.

6 The 1973 Directory for Children's Masses also made provision for a non-ordained adult to preach when the presider or other minister finds it difficult to adapt to the needs of young people in preaching the homily at Mass (24). However, this seems to have been abrogated in the 2004 *Redemptionis Sacramentum*, 65: "It should be borne in mind that any previous norm that may have admitted non-ordained faithful to give the homily during the Eucharistic celebration is to be considered abrogated by the norm of canon 767 §1."

7 Joseph Webb, *Hub symbols: A new approach to effective interpersonal evangelism,* The Center for the Study of Christian Communication, Malibu, 1982.

8 Tom Long, *The Witness of Preaching,* Westminster John Knox Press, St Louis, Missouri, 1989, pp.24-47.

9 Robert Waznak, *An Introduction to the Homily,* Liturgical Press, Collegeville, MN, 1998, chapter 2.

10 Bishops Committee on Priestly Life and Ministry *Fulfilled in your hearing: The Homily in the Sunday Assembly*, United States Conference of Catholic Bishops, Washington D.C., 1982, p. 7.

11 *Fulfilled in your hearing*. 10.

12 *Catechism of the Catholic Church* 1074 and 1349.

13 *Fulfilled in your hearing*, 13.

14 *Fulfilled in your hearing,* 14 and 15.

15 Waznak, Ibid*,* 60.

16 David Fleer and Dave Bland (eds.), *Preaching Autobiography: Connecting the World of the Preacher to the World of the Text,* Rochester College Lectures on Preaching, Vol. 2*.,* ACU Press, Abilene, Texas, 2001, 23-46.

17 Buttrick, D, *Homiletic: Moves and Structures*, Fortress Press, Philadelphia, 1987, 142,

18 (Book 1,11,4-6) appointed as the second reading for the Office of Readings memorial for St Gregory the Great on 3 September.

19 http://mad-eyes.net/disco/tb/papa-dont-preach.htm

20 *Fulfilled in your hearing*, chapter 4.

21 "Ideas for Better Sermons Emerge at Synod: Guidelines and Year of the Homily Proposed" http://www.zenit.org/article-23849?l=english

22 *Christus Dominus*, Decree on the Pastoral Office of Bishops, 13.

23 Benedict XVI, *Sacramentum Caritatis*, 46.

24 L Tubbs Tisdale, *Preaching as Local Theology and Folk Art*, Fortress Press, Minneapolis, 1997 p.23.

25 *Lumen Gentium, Dogmatic Constitution on the Church*, 48-51.

26 Tisdale, Ibid. 39.

27 Reuel L Howe, *Partners in Preaching: Clergy and Laity in Dialogue*, Seabury Press, New York, 1967.

28 *Fulfilled in your hearing*, 7.

29 Ibid. 8.

30 David Buttrick, *Speaking Parables: A Homiletic Guide*, Westminster John Knox Press, Louisville, Kentucky, 2000, 192.

31 *De Trinitate* 1:37-38 Second reading for the Office of Readings for the optional memoria of St Hilary on 13 January in the Roman Breviary.

32 *General Instruction on the Roman Missal*, 55 *and Sacrosanctum Concilium* 7

33 *Fulfilled in your hearing*, chapter 21. 4.

34 *Lectionary for Mass: General Introduction*, 24.

35 Paul A Janowiak, *The Holy Preaching: The Sacramentality of the Word in the Liturgical Assembly*. Collegeville, MN: Liturgical Press, 2000, p17.

36 See chapter 4 of Robert Hendrie's *Go Tell Them; Towards a Theology of Preaching*, St Pauls Publishing, London, 2006.

37 *Fulfilled in your hearing*, 17.

38 Ibid., 10.

39 *The Interpretation of the Bible in the Church*, 1A.

40 *Fulfilled in your hearing*, 17.

41 *The Interpretation of the Bible in the Church* D3.

42 *Fulfilled in your hearing*, 38.

43 *Sacrosanctum Concilium*, Constitution on the Sacred Liturgy, 56, 7, 33 and 52.

44 *Ad Gentes*, Decree on the Missionary Activity of the Church, 6.

45 *Presbyterorum Ordinis*, Decree on the Ministry and Life of Priests, 4.

46 Tom Troeger, *Fresh Images from Preaching,* Judson, Valley Forge, 1982, p.30.

47 Eugene L Lowry, *The Homiletical Plot: The Sermon as Narrative Art Form,* Westminster John Knox Press, 2001, p.121.

48 Geoffrey Hunter, Gethwin Thomas and Stephen Wright, *A Preacher's Companion,* Foreword by James Jones, Bishop of Liverpool, BRF, Oxford, 2004, p.29.

49 "Hermeneutics seems to me to be animated by this double motivation: willingness to suspect, willingness to listen; vow of rigour, vow of obedience." Paul Ricoeur, *Freud and Philosophy: An Essay on Interpretation* New Haven: Yale University Press, 1970.

50 Brown, Raymond, *The Gospel According to John, I-XII,* London: Geoffrey Chapman, 1971, 131-32.

51 Francis J Moloney, Ed. Daniel J Harrington, *The Gospel of John, Sacra Pagina Series,* Collegeville, MN: Liturgical Press, 1998, 92-93.

52 Malina, Bruce J and Rohrbaugh, Richard J, *Social Science Commentary on the Gospel of John,* Minneapolis: Fortress Press, 1998, 81-82.

53 Donahue, John R and Harrington, Daniel J, SJ, Ed. Daniel J Harrington *The Gospel of Mark, Sacra Pagina Series,* Collegeville, MN: Liturgical Press, 1998, 300.

54 Cullmann, Oscar, Baptism in the New Testament, *Studies in Biblical Theology* No. 1, London: SCM Press, 1950, 79.

55 The Numbers reading is given for 26th Sunday in Ordinary Time, Year B in the Roman Lectionary and as an optional alternative for the 18th Sunday after Pentecost in the Revised Common Lectionary. Commentators drawing attention to the parallel include Morna Hooker, *The Gospel According to Saint Mark,* Black's New Testament Commentaries, A and C Black, London 1991, 229 and Daniel Harrington, *The Gospel According to Mark, Jerome Biblical Commentary,* ed. Raymond Brown et al, Geoffrey Chapman, London, 1990 and 98, 616.

56 Donahue, John R, SJ and Harrington, Daniel, SJ, *The Gospel of Mark: Sacra Pagina,* ed. D.J. Harrington, SJ, The Liturgical Press, Collegeville, Minnesota, 2002, 290

57 Henry Wansborough, *Saint Mark, New Catholic Commentary on Holy Scripture,* London, Nelson, 1969, 970.

58 Newman, John H, *Catena Aurea: Commentary on the Four Gospels: Collected out of the Works of the Fathers by Saint Thomas Aquinas, Volume Three, Saint Mark,* The Saint Austin Press, Southampton, England, 1997 (first published in English in 1941), 184.

59 Ibid. 185.
60 For example John Knox: 'What will you do, Papist priests? There rests no sacrifice to be offered for sin by you, nor by any mortal man. These are dolorous tidings unto your hearts. And no marvel! …But the Mass is known not only to be no sacrifice, but also to be idolatry.' *A Vindication of the Doctrine that the Sacrifice of the Mass is Idolatry,* 1550.
61 Chapter IV of *The Decree on Ecclesiastical Hierarchy, and on Ordination* of the Council of Trent, 23rd session, 1563, reproduced in Clarkson, John F, SJ et al, *The Church Teaches, Documents of the Catholic Tradition in Translation,* Tan Books, Rockford, Illinois, 1973, 331.
62 In 1534 the Act of Supremacy confirmed King Henry VIII's status as Supreme Head of the Church of England. Under the Catholic Queen Mary the Act was repealed in 1555. The year after Elizabeth became queen in 1558 the original Act was restored but the title was modified to 'Supreme Governor'.
63 *Apostolicae Curae, On the Nullity of Anglican Orders,* Promulgated September 18, 1896 by Pope Leo XIII, Para 6 36.
64 *How My Mind Has Changed* Richard A McCormick, SJ. This article is one in a series from the *Christian Century* magazine prepared for *Religion on Line.*
65 Decree on Ecumenism *Unitatis Redintegratio,* Chapter 1, paragraph 3.
66 Ibid, Chapter III, paragraph 13.
67 Ibid, Chapter III , paragraph 23.
68 Church of Ireland Response Adopted by the Committee for Christian Unity, Received by the Standing Committee of the General Synod: "Sister Churches": Responding to "Dominus Jesus" and the "Note" from the Congregation for the Doctrine of the Faith.
69 *The Tablet,* July 14, p.33. This report also includes reference to more generous interpretations of the Roman document by Archbishop Rowan Williams and by the eminent British Methodist preacher, Lord Leslie Griffiths.
70 Although Christian Palestinians make up 6.7% of the total of Palestinians throughout the world, the numbers in the West Bank and Gaza now stand at 2.9% and in Israel at 2.3% in a society that has a 14% Palestinian minority. In Jerusalem the Christian population more than halved between 1914 and 1981 and has steadily declined since.
71 Modern Palestinian society is changing dramatically under Western influences. The early stages of this change

are described in Schöleh, Alexander, 1993 *Palestine in Transformation, 1856-1882*, Studies in Economic and Social, Economic and Political Development, Institute for Palestine Studies, Washington DC.

72 e.g., Matthew 4:8-22, Matthew 22:1:28, and Luke 15:11-32.

73 e.g., Matthew 1:18-25.

74 Luke 16:18.

75 Matthew 11:19 and Luke 7:37-39.

76 John 8:3-4.

77 Mark 12:7 and Luke 15:11.

78 Christian Palestinians have had similar laws administered by Church Courts as part of the *Millet* system from Ottoman times.

79 e.g. Luke 16:1-9.

80 Adding together the figures for Israel and the West Bank and Gaza, the Greek Orthodox are the largest Christian community with around 55,000. The Greek Catholics have around 53,000, the Latins more than 38,000, the Maronites 6,000, Anglicans and Lutherans combine to about 3,000 and the Armenians about 2,000.

81 For a discussion of this term see Wilken, R.L., 1992. *The Land called Holy. Palestine in Christian History and Thought.* Yale: Yale University Press, p.92.

82 Palestinians use the Arabic word *Al Naqba*, meaning 'Calamity' to describe the events of 1948.

83 John 11:39.